RED
REDEMPTION

RED
REDEMPTION

How Aberdeen Ended a
35-Year Wait for Scottish Cup Glory

R Y A N   C R O M B I E

pitch

First published by Pitch Publishing, 2026

1

pitch

Pitch Publishing
9 Donnington Park,
85 Birdham Road,
Chichester, West Sussex,
PO20 7AJ
www.pitchpublishing.co.uk
info@pitchpublishing.co.uk

A CIP catalogue record is available for this book
from the British Library.

ISBN 978 1 83680 415 4

Typesetting and origination by Pitch Publishing

MIX
Paper | Supporting
responsible forestry
FSC
www.fsc.org   FSC™ C016779

Printed and bound on FSC® certified paper in line with
our continuing commitment to ethical business practices,
sustainability and the environment.

Printed and bound in India by Replika Press Pvt. Ltd.

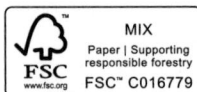

Contents

For my dad and grandad,
my Gothenburg Greats

Acknowledgements

LIKE SO many of you reading this, I am not afraid to admit that I have an obsession with football and, in particular, Aberdeen Football Club. For that, I have my dad to thank, or rather blame, and he, in turn, can thank my grandad for imbuing the spirit of the Dons within him. My first time watching Aberdeen was when I was just three years old – a 2-1 win over St Mirren at Pittodrie in 2000. I can't say I remember much about that game, but I am reliably informed that I got a fright when Aberdeen scored. Alas, I cannot claim to have attended Pittodrie during the 20th century, where all of the old stadium's best memories linger. I am one of those Aberdeen fans who have been raised on the stories of the glory years. Growing up, my dad was treated to Fergie, league titles, innumerable Scottish Cup successes, and he and my grandad were even in Gothenburg. I, on the other hand, well, I got mediocrity, Queen of the South, Hampden hammerings, and regular cup disappointments. Regardless, as a trio, we travelled the country following the Dons. In those days, the closest we came to silverware was when my grandad used to twist and bend his toffee wrappers into little trophies for me at half-time.

Among all of the disappointments, there were the gems that made it all worth it. Watching Aberdeen dismantle

Copenhagen at Pittodrie with both of them sitting either side of me remains one of my favourite games. As the years rolled on, unfortunately my grandad, a sufferer from the cruel Parkinson's disease, saw his health deteriorate, and we started watching games from the disabled section at Pittodrie and then latterly from the comfort of his living room. The last time I saw him before he went into hospital, we were sitting, watching Aberdeen versus Motherwell on the television – the Dons won 2-0. Me and my dad carried on the mantle, and in the ten years since, from Rijeka to Rugby Park, we had pretty much seen it all together – apart from lifting the Scottish Cup.

* * *

Now, it's time for a small confession. I was born and raised in Edinburgh and am one of those football fans who follow their dad's team rather than their local one. I vehemently rejected the notion of supporting either of the Edinburgh clubs – the north-east was in my blood. And, at just one year old, I was Aberdeen's number one dribbler, so my baby bib said anyway. The point of revealing this dark secret was that I and my dad regularly posited that for Aberdeen to lift the Scottish Cup once again, at least one of us needed to live there – he had left the Granite City with my grandma and grandad in 1986. We concluded that it was that, and not the departure of Fergie or the advent of commercialisation in football, which heralded Aberdeen's fall from glory – 1990 being the exception that proved the rule. So, when the wheels were set in motion for me to move up to Aberdeen in early May 2025, it was a theory we were able to put to the test. In the end, I and my girlfriend Jess, along with our dog Nellie, moved into our new house on 16 May. A week later the Dons were Scottish Cup winners.

As football fans, we often look for patterns where there are none, and many of you will undoubtedly have similar anecdotes. I do know deep down that it is not the estate agent or mortgage broker that I have to thank for 24 May, but Jimmy Thelin and the players. They gave us one of the greatest days of our lives with that performance at Hampden, and, although they put us through the wringer over the course of the season, they came out the other side as heroes. I will be up front and say that this book does not contain any interviews with those players or indeed the manager who spirited the Scottish Cup back north, but it was never my intention to do so – they have said all that they will say, at least until their careers are over. What made this cup win so special was because of what it meant to the club, its supporters and a whole city, and I have tried to capture that over the course of these pages – I hope this book does the story justice.

My eternal thanks go to those who have contributed to this book and brought it to life. In alphabetical order, they are: Adam Rooney, Beth Wallace, Brian Sloan, Charlie Rowley, Darren Abel, Dave Cormack, Duncan Milne, Frederic Fendrich, Gilbert Falconer, Glen Schreuder, Graham Spiers, Gus Tawse, Joe Lewis, Joel Besseling, John Hughes, Kathleen Gray, Kieren Joseph, Lewis Birrell, Mats Gren, Matt Findlay, Michael Duncan, Michael Grant, Richard Caldicott, Roderick Murray, Rory Hamilton, Stephen McCormick, Stewart Smith.

I'd like to extend my special thanks to Aberdeen FC Hall of Fame inductee Brian Irvine for generously donating his valuable time to be interviewed and for providing the foreword to the book. It was an honour to have someone who sits inside the top ten all-time appearance list for the club to put his name behind the project.

I'd also like to thank Jane Camillin at Pitch Publishing for agreeing to let me write about something I have always dreamed about, and Duncan Olner for the front cover design.

My immeasurable thanks to my family for their continued support throughout both this project and my career. A special thank you to my dad for serving as a sounding board for much of this content. I'm sure I can pay you back in Pittodrie Pies.

A huge thank you to my girlfriend Jess, who has allowed me to burrow myself away in front of my computer for three months and supported me every step of the way throughout the process – I could not have done it without her love and support.

And finally, thank you to you for picking up this book. If you are of a Dons persuasion, I hope that you enjoy it and that it rekindles those memories of that unforgettable day in May 2025. If you are not, I hope you enjoy the story. It's quite something.

Foreword
by Brian Irvine

LIKE THE thousands of Dons fans who travelled to Hampden for the 2025 Scottish Cup Final, and the many more who watched or listened from afar, I felt a real sense of anticipation and excitement ahead of the game. But with that came fear, too. Facing Celtic at Hampden always brings a challenge, and after 35 years without lifting the trophy, the hope was simply that Aberdeen would do the city proud. As it turned out, they did much more than that.

After a solid performance and, remarkably, a relatively stress-free penalty shoot-out (unlike in 1990!), Aberdeen finally brought the Scottish Cup back to the Granite City. On a personal note it was a special day, not just because of what it meant to the club, but also because it coincided with my 60th birthday. It was also fitting that the journey began against Elgin City – the only club I managed after my playing career ended. That little detail made the story feel even more personal to me. Looking back now, it really does feel like our name was on the cup in 2025.

For me, the 2025 win stirred memories of our own triumph in 1990. As I watched Graeme Shinnie lift the trophy, I couldn't help but reflect on how different – and yet how familiar – it all felt. In 1990, I walked up to take my penalty, feeling oddly confident knowing that I had a kick to win the cup and had Theo Snelders to thank for saving the penalty before. In 2025, after Celtic missed their first penalty, Aberdeen's shoot-out felt strangely calm. Every player stepped up to the occasion. It was as if the pressure had been lifted – not just from the team, but from an entire city.

What stood out most that day was the wall of red in the stands. Seeing a 50-50 split at Hampden is rare these days, but Aberdeen fans filled their half with colour, voice and belief. And by the end, it felt like the entirety of the stadium belonged to them. Those scenes brought home just how much this club means to the north-east – and how deeply the people of Aberdeen feel its triumphs and struggles.

This book tells the story of that long journey – the false dawns, the heartbreaks, the near-misses, and yes, the lows of the numerous cup shocks – that made the joy of 2025 so special. It's been a rollercoaster since 1990, but this win brought pride flooding back to a city and fanbase long starved of glory – and with it, a new cast of heroes to carry the story forward.

As a Dons fan myself, it is a great privilege to contribute this foreword to *Red Redemption: How Aberdeen Ended a 35-Year Wait for Scottish Cup Glory*. I hope you enjoy reliving that unforgettable moment and that it brings back the same pride and emotion that it gave me.

Brian Irvine
Aberdeen, Scotland

Prologue

IT IS often said that a week is a long time in football. What, then, is 35 years? An eternity? For an answer, head to the north-east of Scotland. Pressed between the granite sprawl of the city and the restless North Sea, you'll find Pittodrie, the traditional home of Aberdeen Football Club. If you are sitting in the cantilever South Stand, the cold wind batters you from both sides and, on a clear afternoon the North Sea is visible on the horizon behind the looming Richard Donald Stand. You wouldn't think it, looking at it now, but these parts used to be home to the best team in Europe. The great Bayern Munich were once laid low out on that very pitch as Sir Alex Ferguson beamed in the dugout. In 1985, Willie Miller all but retained the league title with his famous stooping header against Celtic at the Merkland Road End. It was a time when the Dons ruled Scotland and, for a period, Europe. Throughout the 1980s, just as the oil did, league titles, Scottish Cups and European trophies flowed into the Granite City in abundance. When a fresh-faced Alex Ferguson arrived at Pittodrie in 1978, the Dons had won the Scottish Cup just twice across their 75-year history. By the time he departed for the grandeur of Manchester United in 1986, he had tripled that haul to six. Between 1982 and 1985, fearless captain Miller lifted the trophy three years in succession – a feat matched only by Celtic in the 40 years since. The good times were not to last.

By 2025 the Scottish Cup, once a regular visitor to Aberdeen, had now not set foot in these parts for 35 years. It pained everyone with a connection to the club. Over the course of its history, Scotland's national cup competition has been predominantly dominated by two sides. As of April 2025, Celtic and Rangers had won a combined 76 trophies from the 139 times it had been contested. Outside of the halcyon days of the 80s, the green and blue sides of Glasgow have played a game of 'to me, to you' with the country's three major honours. You have to go as far back as 1955 for the last time both clubs endured trophyless campaigns in the same season. In that remarkable year, Aberdeen, under the auspices of manager Dave Halliday, claimed their first league title, Clyde clinched their second Scottish Cup, while Hearts won the tenth edition of the League Cup.

That was 70 years ago now, and the stark reality is that Glasgow's stranglehold – Celtic's in particular – on the Scottish game has only become ever tighter. Since the turn of the millennium, Celtic have racked up a dozen Scottish Cups, half of those coming as part of a domestic treble, underlining just how difficult it is for the so-called provincial clubs to win silverware in this era. The sun has well and truly set on the days of the underdog in Scotland.

And yet, Scottish Cup Final day continues to carry enormous weight within the national game. While the allure of the FA Cup has faded somewhat south of the border, the Scottish Cup maintains its pride of place as the end-of-season showpiece occasion. Its significance is equalled by few other fixtures in the Scottish football calendar. For the supporters, it's a competition that conjures up emotions rarely experienced in any other walk of life. Ecstasy, jubilation, heartbreak and sorrow – this competition delivers it all. For those who have been lucky enough to see their side reach the final, Hampden beckons. For the majority on the outside looking in, an afternoon in the pub, in front of the television or listening on the radio awaits. It's a day when new heroes are crowned, hearts are broken and names become etched into club folklore, immortalised, to be remembered evermore. In May 2025 Brendan Rodgers's insatiable Celtic were eyeing up yet another clean sweep of the silverware, with just the Scottish Cup left to claim. Standing in their way? Aberdeen.

Saturday, 24 May 2025

It's 1.30pm. On the west side of Hampden Park lie the neighbourhoods of Battlefield and Shawlands. On a usual Saturday, it's an area that hums with the relaxed atmosphere of locals idling between independent coffee shops, bakeries and brunch spots. Today it's a bit different. It's teeming with Aberdeen supporters. Why? It's Scottish Cup Final day. Aberdeen versus Celtic.

One such venue which has been taken over by the masses of Aberdonians is Church on the Hill, a converted church turned gastropub in the heart of Langside, just a 15-minute walk from Hampden. It's bursting at the seams. Red and white is crammed into every nook and cranny. Inside, the bar is an impenetrable wall of bodies, a five-row-deep scrum where reaching the front is a 30-minute mission. The poor souls working behind it must have been cursing the rota for landing them on such an unrelenting shift. The mood among the Aberdeen fans is upbeat, good-humoured, and the vast majority are enjoying a pre-match singsong, encouraged by one or two libations.

As kick-off approaches, the conversations invariably turn towards the match itself. The consensus within the Dons support seems to be that pre-match pints and a chinwag with old friends is going to be the highlight of the day – the football is an added inconvenience. A conversation happening to the right of the bar rather sums up the attitude towards the game itself. 'If it gets to four, I'm coming back to the pub,' says one of the group. Nobody even argues a case against that scenario. If anything, the others nod in agreement that they would be joining him. Gloominess and pessimism are traits that are continuously labelled at Aberdonians.

On this occasion, their scepticism seemed warranted. In the preceding month Aberdeen had concluded the final weeks of their league campaign in galling fashion, which included a 5-1 mauling by Celtic at Pittodrie. It was a stake to the heart of their hopes of upsetting the odds in this Scottish Cup Final. The previous meeting between the sides at the national stadium had resulted in a rout, Aberdeen's unbeaten start to the season ending in ignominious fashion as they were embarrassed 6-0. Furthermore, Aberdeen had lost each of their last ten matches against Celtic at Hampden, the last victory coming in a League Cup semi-final in September 1992, when Eoin Jess netted the winner. Who then can blame the fans who had descended on Glasgow's south side for steeling themselves against what was expected to be another bruising afternoon at the national stadium?

Fifteen minutes later, a sudden hush falls over the pub as the Aberdeen fans digest the team news on their mobile phones as a collective. The amateur analysts among the support propose that their manager has shaken things up and opted for a back five, with young centre-back Jack Milne a surprise inclusion in the starting 11. Aberdeen's Swedish gaffer, Jimmy Thelin, has rolled the dice, deviating from the 4-2-3-1 formation he had yet to waver from all season. With the team news announced, the vast majority inside the pub decide it's their cue to leave. Outside, a torrent of red is sweeping towards the national stadium.

Pain, agony, humiliation and misery paved Aberdeen's 35-year Scottish Cup journey to the 2025 final. Once more, the Red Army was walking the familiar path towards a stadium that renders nothing but heartbreak for an entire generation of Dons fans. Whether numbed by past experiences or having already resigned themselves to their fate, the travelling Aberdonians were in surprisingly good spirits. Chants of 'Stand Free' and 'Aberdeen Olé Olé Olé' punctured the Glasgow air, the singing growing louder and louder the closer you got to Hampden. As the undulating roof of the national stadium came into view, so did a vast sea of red and white below it. Thousands upon thousands of people clad in every shade of red imaginable swarmed around the stadium, announcing their arrival at this Scottish Cup Final. Red top after red top swivelled through the turnstiles, leaving fear and inhibitions at the threshold. Hampden has its faults, but the way in which the vast bowl arena opens up in front of you as you walk up the steps stirs something special in the soul. On this of all days, it was a sight to behold.

From the halfway line at the North Stand, all the way round the West Stand and into the corporate seats in Hampden's South Stand, was a wall of red. Aberdeen's ultras group had launched their simple 'All in Red' campaign in the weeks leading up to the final, urging Dons fans to wear the club's colours to the final. As the Dons' end-of-season run stumbled and came to a crashing halt, the media hastened to write off any notion of an Aberdeen victory in this final. Some had suggested that their fans need not even bother making the journey south. As such, the 'All in Red' campaign assumed the form of a last stand of defiance at Hampden. Aberdeen might go down, but the fans weren't willing to do so without a fight. This thin red line was no thin line at all but was bursting with 20,000 raucous Aberdonians. As is so often the case, the Red Army had answered the call. Now it was over to the team to do the same.

Inside the Hampden tunnel, Brendan Rodgers stands poised to lead his all-conquering Celtic side on to the pitch, his players ready to bask in the acclaim and complete a historic treble. To his left, his opposite number, Jimmy Thelin, cuts a far quieter figure. This Aberdeen team is ready to write its own story.

1

The Class of 1990

UP UNTIL Jimmy Thelin's arrival in the north-east of Scotland, just ten of Aberdeen's previous 25 full-time managers had steered the Dons to the Scottish Cup Final. Of those, only four had ever returned to the Granite City with the trophy. Thelin, then, having reached the final in his inaugural season at Pittodrie, was already one of a select few to have done so. If he could go one step further, he would take his place in a pantheon of which the only four members were Dave Halliday, Eddie Turnbull, Alex Ferguson and Alex Smith. If it were inspiration from past glories that the Swede was in search of in his quest to join that famed quartet, then he'd have had to dig deep into the Pittodrie archives.

The last time Aberdeen Football Club got their hands on the Scottish Cup, the world wide web didn't exist, the Soviet Union was still a country, and the legendary Willie Miller, now 70 years old, was still on the books as a player. Those were different times – so different in fact that Aberdeen swaggered up to Hampden on 12 May 1990 as favourites against a struggling Celtic, something barely comprehensible in these modern times. Such was Aberdeen's relentless nature throughout the 80s, they established themself as Scotland's top dogs. Sir Alex Ferguson dedicated his eight years at the club to hammering, sometimes literally, belief into his players that they could go to Glasgow and dethrone the Old Firm on their own patch. Ferguson may have departed the Dons, but his everlasting legacy was that Aberdeen, once the modest, unpresuming club from the north-east coast, was a force to be reckoned with. Yet after Fergie's departure in 1986 the club was reeling with the loss of its greatest manager and the death of its vice-chairman and visionary, Chris Anderson. It subsequently stumbled through three trophyless years.

However, they ended the drought, and it *was* a drought by 1980s Aberdeen standards, claiming the 1989/90 season's first piece of silverware. They had reached the League Cup Final for the third consecutive year, facing off against Rangers, just as they had in the previous two years, losing out on both occasions. The supporters could barely stomach a third successive cup final loss to their bitter rivals. Thankfully, the third time proved a charm as Alex Smith's team downed Rangers 2-1 after extra time, some form of revenge on Graeme Souness's men. Despite the three-year silverware shortage, Alex Smith's first trophy at Pittodrie lifted the club's tally of major honours since 1980 to an astonishing 11, more than any other team in Scotland over the same period. It was no surprise then that the feeling in the build-up to the 1990 cup final was one of confidence from the Dons.

'Aberdeen would just have to choose what has become the year of the underdog to go into today's Scottish Cup Final as favourites against a Celtic side desperate to rescue a season which has brought mostly frustration and failure,' wrote the *Press and Journal* on the morning of the big game.

Canvassing opinions for its cup final preview, the *Dundee Courier* summarised that 'the way some people are talking Aberdeen only need to turn up for today's Scottish Cup Final to win the trophy'.

The notion that the final was a foregone conclusion was in part because a much-changed Aberdeen had swept aside the Hoops at Celtic Park with ease just a week prior. Youngsters Graham Watson and Eoin Jess were on the scoresheet as Aberdeen ran out 3-1 winners in a comfortable evening in Glasgow. The match, the final one of the league season, saw Celtic confined to a fifth-placed finish. Symptomatic of Celtic's season, it ended a torrid campaign in which they had lost more games than they had won and finished just four points above ninth-placed St Mirren – Glasgow's east-enders hadn't had their troubles to seek, and the supporters were restless. Aberdeen were eager to pile on the misery as they chased their own piece of history – a famous cup double was within touching distance.

With the quality and experience of Hans Gillhaus, Charlie Nicholas and Jim Bett all expected to return to the side after being rested for the Parkhead encounter, the Dons were odds-on favourites to do so. Smith was rightly in a confident mood ahead of the game: 'We've heard all about Celtic's troubles but we'll have to be at our best to lift the cup. It will be difficult, but we have a lot of quality players with experience of this situation. If they play to their best form the cup ours.' The Aberdeen support shared their manager's view that, if their team turned up, they would lift the trophy. Fuelled by years of Fergie rhetoric, some Dons fans were less effusive of the opposition, one writing into the *Press and Journal* in the build-up to the big match, 'It's obvious Aberdeen are going to win. I have the feeling it could be their year. If the Dons play to form, Celtic don't have a chance, even though the game is being played in their own backyard.'

The fact that Aberdeen's allocation of 23,500 tickets was snapped up in a single day pointed to the widespread expectation among the supporters. The days of the Dons being intimidated on their travels to Hampden to face one of the Old Firm were gone. The club's lionhearted captain, Willie Miller, was the cornerstone of that mentality shift throughout the 1980s. If there were indeed any doubts about Aberdeen's chances when the teams took to the Hampden surface on 12 May, it would be because they did so without their moustachioed mountain. Miller, an ever-present at the heart of the defence, had captained the team to their last 12 major honours but would be forced to watch on from the stands on this occasion. Despite featuring in that 3-1 win at Celtic, Miller was still short of full fitness as he continued to recover from the serious knee injury he had sustained on international duty in November. Nevertheless, Aberdeen were still able to form an impressive backline – Brian Irvine had been a capable deputy during Miller's absence, while Alex McLeish picked up the Scottish Football Writers' Association Player of the Year award for the season. They were flanked by the personification of consistency in the way of Stewart McKimmie and David Robertson.

The game itself proved a lacklustre affair. In keeping with the majority of pre-match predictions, it was Aberdeen who exerted the greater share of control, albeit with little end product. Aberdeen's best chance came in the opening minutes when Charlie Nicholas wriggled free to create some space for himself in the box, but his powerful drive was blocked on the line. The predicted procession to the trophy failed to materialise, and nerves began to grip the expectant Dons support. The golden opportunity to clinch a famous cup double for just the second time in the club's history was in jeopardy, and referee George Smith blew for full time with the teams locked at 0-0. Extra time, in which Aberdeen had become renowned for showcasing their superior fitness over the last decade, passed by without incident. So, as if destined from the start, the showpiece occasion would be decided by penalties – a first for the competition. The controversial motion to introduce penalties to settle the final was passed overwhelmingly at the Scottish Football Association's annual meeting in 1989. As both sets of players crowded round their respective managers, a dread had set in among the Dons support on the west side of Hampden. Aberdeen had a loathsome relationship with spot-kicks. The Dons had been the first team to be knocked out of European competition on penalties when they were beaten by Budapest Honvéd in the first round of the 1970/71 European Cup Winners' Cup. They had also lost the League Cup Final to Rangers in agonising fashion in 1987. Naturally, the tension inside Hampden ramped up.

Once both teams had finished their final preparations and the five penalty takers had been decided, a toss of the coin saw that the spot-kicks would be taken in front of the Aberdeen fans in the West Stand. Celtic's Polish left-back Darriusz Wdowczyk was the first to step forward. Whether because of the Hampden sunshine or the big, towering Dutchman Theo Snelders in between the sticks, Wdowczyk never looked comfortable. His floundering run-up preceded a side-footed strike which flew wide of the goal. Snelders, sporting a bold yellow-and-black goalkeeper top, leapt to his feet, clenching his fists in delight. A roar went up from the Dons fans, whose pre-shoot-out worries were alleviated in an instant.

Jim Bett was first in line for Aberdeen and he sumptuously slotted his kick into the corner past the helpless Packie Bonner. Aberdeen were in the driving seat in the shoot-out. Celtic's response, however, was faultless as Peter Grant, Paul McStay and Tommy Coyne all found the net. Bobby Connor and Hans Gillhaus scored for the Dons to put the cup within touching distance. Brian Grant, a staple in the Aberdeen side throughout the season, stepped up and blazed his strike over the bar. The 35,000 Celtic fans let out an almighty cry as they sensed that this was the moment that their torrid season would turn on its head. A marathon of penalties ensued in which it seemed as if there was a magnet inside the ball, dragging it into the net. Ten penalties, five apiece, were converted in succession before boyhood Celtic supporter Anton Rogan made the long walk to the penalty area. Even by the standards of the time, Rogan's run-up was so comically long that he may as well have stayed at the halfway line and asked the referee to spot the ball for him. It telegraphed which side of the goal he was aiming for. Snelders leapt to his left and, extending his body to its limit, reached out a hand to tip Rogan's effort wide of the post. In what is now an iconic image, the Dutch goalkeeper, just as he had done with Celtic's first missed penalty, leapt to his feet, fists pumping as he joined the Aberdeen support in wild celebration.

However, the Dons still had a penalty to score. The monumental task fell to Brian Irvine. 'When I was walking forward to take the penalty, I was thinking that this is the one to win it and I actually felt myself getting more and more confident with every step as I was walking from the halfway line,' said Irvine. 'I knew this was my chance to be a hero for Aberdeen. As I swung my foot, I remember immediately seeing the Celtic goalkeeper move left. I'd put the ball down the middle and was just relieved.' In that moment, Irvine shouldered a responsibility as weighty as any borne by the man they call 'God' in the Granite City. And he came out the other side a legend. 'All the credit has to go to Theo [Snelders] for making the great save just before my penalty. It took the pressure off me completely. I am not joking when I say that if my penalty had been earlier and I had to score to keep us in it, I probably would have missed. I wasn't confident about taking penalties at all. It was a dream come true to score the winning penalty for my boyhood club.'

As the ball hit the back of the net, Irvine simply stood on the penalty spot with his arms outstretched in celebration before he was embraced and lifted to the sky in triumph by Snelders. It was the tallest he had ever felt. 'The celebrations in the aftermath were every bit as good. I can remember it all, clearly thinking, did that really just happen? The next day, we headed back to Aberdeen and changed buses just outside of the city on to the open-top bus. I vividly remember coming up Union Street with people everywhere, waving their flags and cheering. It was undoubtedly the best memory I have at the club.'

The media reaction in the aftermath was awash with praise for an Aberdeen side that had, in the end, delivered on the expectations placed upon them. 'Hopefully this can be the catalyst to take us to the Premier Division championship,' beamed a delighted Alex Smith. Aberdeen were the irrefutable cup kings of Scotland, and you couldn't blame the man who had led them there for his boldness. The swift shift in focus to the upcoming league campaign said it all – winning trophies at Pittodrie had become an expectation; anything else was deemed as failure. The Scottish Cup marked Aberdeen's 12th honour in just ten years. Before 1980 they had lifted only five across their 87-year history. Now trips to Hampden to dispatch either half of the Old Firm and return north with silverware had become regular occurrences. With a trophy cabinet bursting at the seams, success at Aberdeen felt inevitable in those days. These were the club's undisputed golden days. 'That team was something special,' said Irvine. 'Alex Ferguson's Aberdeen sides in the early 80s came together like a cake – it was the perfect mix of ingredients, and that side in 1990 was the same. The club had unbelievable momentum from the success of the 80s, and it felt like we were just continuing in the same way.'

However, by nature, golden days are not eternal. They were not to know it, but as the Aberdeen fans watched Irvine sweep his cup-winning penalty into the back of the net, they were witnessing the end of an era. As the red-and-white mass celebrated on the Hampden terraces, the long wait had already begun.

2

The Wilderness Years

GIVEN THEIR success in the competition throughout the second half of the 20th century, there was a time when mention of the Scottish Cup would spark a gleam in the eye of Aberdeen supporters. For those who lived through the 80s, it was a competition synonymous with success, delivering a seemingly endless catalogue of joyful memories. Such was the regularity with which captain Willie Miller lifted the trophy, it seemed as though it had become welded to his iconic right hand. The red juggernaut from the north-east had utterly shattered the established order of the Glasgow duopoly, which dominated Scottish football. At the turn of the 90s, Scottish football had become so accustomed to seeing its trophies adorned in red and white ribbons, nobody would have envisaged the long barren spell which was to follow. As such, in more recent times, the Scottish Cup has become a subject on which Dons fans would rather not dwell.

Aberdeen followed up their 1990 triumph with disappointing back-to-back third-round exits under manager Alex Smith. It was the first time in the club's history that they had failed to progress through a single round of the tournament for two years in succession. The board and supporters had come to demand success, and come February 1992, with the team languishing mid-table and having been dumped out the cup by fierce rivals Rangers, Smith became the first ever manager to be sacked by the club. Willie Miller took up the position, looking to restore the relentless winning mentality that had defined the entirety of his playing career.

In truth, Miller started his managerial career handicapped, his legendary status in the north-east placing an unrealistic burden of expectation upon him. His team certainly restored pride but they could do little in the face of a fiscally charged Rangers, finishing runners-up to the Glasgow side in all three domestic cup competitions in 1992/93, which included a deflating 2-1 Scottish Cup Final defeat. A decade had now passed since Aberdeen's sensational Gothenburg success, and even though the club had clinched a cup double at the beginning of the 90s it was clear that the power the Dons had once wielded within Scottish football was on the wane. 'Miller was desperate to be as successful an Aberdeen manager as he was as a player,' explained Brian Irvine, a cornerstone of the team throughout the 1990s. 'However, just as Alex Ferguson walked the fine line between winning and losing throughout the 80s, more often than not coming out on the winning side, Miller did the opposite during his time in charge.'

The commercialisation of football in the early 90s heralded a new era for the game, with obscene amounts of money beginning to flow to a select group of bigger clubs while the rest became ostracised. It signalled the end for the likes of Aberdeen to be able to dine at the top table of European football. Alex Ferguson's sides were littered with international talent, but in this new age, the club could no longer attract that level of player. 'With the signings Miller was able to bring in, it was clear that it wasn't at the same level as what Aberdeen fans had become used to over the last ten years,' said Irvine. 'They were still great players in and around the dressing room, but not at an international level.'

With Rangers sanctioning unprecedented levels of spending in Scottish football, they exerted a grip on the game unlike any had managed before. It was impossible for Aberdeen to keep pace. Winning trophies was no longer just about the mentality and ability of the 11 players on the football pitch, and the standards that Ferguson had set at the club became impossible to maintain. Off the field, Aberdeen had enjoyed their best years under the stewardship of Dick Donald as chairman and Chris Anderson as vice-chairman. In his 1999 autobiography *Managing My Life*, Ferguson wrote, 'As chairman [Dick Donald] was a colossus and nobody had to tell me that I had little chance of ever working for his like again ... The quality of men Aberdeen had drawn together was remarkable, and there was never a hint of unrest from the boardroom.'

The untimely death of Anderson in 1986 hit the club hard, while the indomitable Donald passed away in 1993. Dick's son Ian took on the reins as chairman after serving on the board for some time but struggled to maintain the cohesiveness and decisiveness that had come to define Aberdeen over the last decade – the Dons began to slide. By the mid-1990s the decline had become apparent: the 1994/95 season saw Aberdeen suffer one of the worst results in Scottish Cup history as they were humbled at Ochilview by third-tier Stenhousemuir, losing out 2-0. 'I was on the bench, so I can't claim much responsibility,' said Irvine. 'I remember watching it thinking, "Oh no, what is going on here?" It was an absolute nightmare. The pitch was heavy, and nobody expected that to happen. One minute you could be playing a top European side, and the next you're struggling against Stenhousemuir. It was a horrendous day.' It was a result that sent shockwaves through Scottish football and was one that was widely considered the darkest day in the history of the club. Part-timers had downed the once-mighty Dons. Already reeling after sacking club legend Willie Miller earlier in the season, with the side languishing second-bottom of the Premier Division, the result sent the club into a tailspin.

By 1999, Aberdeen, now under the interim management of Paul Hegarty following the departure of Alex Miller – who had taken over after Keith Burkinshaw's caretaker spell, which came after Roy Aitken's two and a half years in charge – were struggling badly. Results had gradually begun to improve following the appointment of Hegarty; however, the brief whiff of optimism was almost instantly extinguished. Aberdeen had fallen at the first possible hurdle in the Scottish Cup in each of the last two years and a home tie against third-tier Livingston in January 1999 looked like the perfect opportunity to kickstart what had been a campaign wrought with disappointment. However, their plight lurched into a pit of horrific proportions as the Second Division side left Pittodrie with a 1-0 victory and a place in the next round. Hegarty, ashen-faced in the aftermath, was stunned by the result: 'I am embarrassed, upset and annoyed and I hope the players feel the same.' Although Hegarty somewhat recovered to steer the club clear of the dreaded drop, the board decided against offering him the job on a permanent basis. Utterly disillusioned, the Aberdeen faithful yearned for a new direction, prompting the Pittodrie hierarchy, for the first time, to seek their next leader from beyond the British Isles.

Experienced Dane Ebbe Skovdahl was chosen as the man to breathe new life into the club and was appointed as Aberdeen's next permanent manager that summer. However, with the club's purse strings tightly drawn and a supposed paltry sum of only £2m available to attract new talent, results failed to improve. The Dons won only one of their opening 15 matches, that being an unbelievable 6-5 victory over Motherwell at Fir Park in which they had been 5-2 ahead. A mid-season rally materialised before it all fell off a cliff in March 2000.

Aberdeen finished bottom of the table for only the second time in the club's history, but they would not be relegated. The round-robin play-off format that was set to take place between the Dons, Falkirk and Dunfermline, as a result of the league moving to 12 teams the following season, was ditched. Falkirk's Brockville did not meet the SPL stadia criteria so Aberdeen retained their position in the top flight while Dunfermline and St Mirren were promoted. Despite the ignominy of finishing last, Skovdahl's Aberdeen saved their best performances for cup football, making it to both the League Cup Final and the Scottish Cup Final in the same season. It was as far as they would go. Having already been comfortably defeated 2-0 by Celtic in the League Cup in the first of those finals, Aberdeen were given no chance of overcoming Rangers in the Scottish Cup Final, given their opponents had romped to the league title by 21 points. As the Aberdeen support headed to Hampden expecting the worst, the only shred of hope that they could cling on to was that they had already beaten Rangers in a cup competition that season – a 1-0 win at Pittodrie in the League Cup quarter-final.

That faint hope was quickly crushed almost as soon as the game got under way; after just two minutes, Jim

Leighton was clattered by Rangers striker Rod Wallace, who lunged for the ball in the box and caught him in the face. The veteran had bravely thrown himself on it to prevent Wallace from turning home an early cross, suffering a hefty blow in doing so. The force of the collision fractured his jaw. Leighton lay sprawled on the deck in agony for seven minutes before eventually being carried off on a stretcher. With no substitute goalkeeper on the bench in those days, Skovdahl was forced to play striker Robbie Winters in between the sticks for almost the entirety of the match. Rangers cantered to a 4-0 victory. It was Leighton's final competitive appearance, the 41-year-old hanging up his gloves for good after the game. Over the course of his career he had climbed the Hampden steps four times as an Aberdeen player to lift the Scottish Cup. Now, in his last outing for the club, he was carried down the Hampden tunnel, never to return. The poignant end to a glittering career of one of the Gothenburg Greats seemed to encapsulate Aberdeen's current plight. The triumphs of the 1980s had faded into little more than distant echoes as the club struggled to come to terms with the new era of football.

After Skovdahl's eventual departure in 2002, the board hired Steve Paterson, who was viewed as one of the most promising young managers in Scotland at the time. Paterson had overseen great success at Inverness Caledonian Thistle, including the famous victory at Parkhead, where his side went ballistic and Celtic were atrocious. However, severe personal issues had Paterson on a collision course with disaster. Within three months of joining the Dons he failed to turn up for a game against Dundee following a night of heavy drinking. With Aberdeen finishing in a grim 11th spot at the end of the 2003/04 season, he was sacked and left

Pittodrie in the boot of a car to avoid the waiting press. It was an ill-fated spell in both the club and Paterson's history, and both looked to move on quickly.

The start of the new millennium had been rather painful for the Aberdeen support, with the club finishing inside the bottom two twice in just five years. Hammerings away to rivals and early cup exits had suddenly become the norm – it was a sad decline. Succeeding Paterson, and desperately seeking to change the fortunes of the Dons, was Jimmy Calderwood, arriving from Dunfermline Athletic after a successful five years in Fife. Calderwood galvanised the club during his time at the helm, dragging it from the depths of the division's bottom half and re-establishing it as a contender towards the top end of the table where it belonged. In his five years in the Granite City, Calderwood guided Aberdeen to finishes of fourth, sixth, third and twice fourth, while also delivering some famous European nights – none more memorable than the 4-0 demolition of Copenhagen at Pittodrie.

However, if Skohvdal had cracked the cups at the expense of the league, Calderwood was working in reverse. Aberdeen suffered heavy defeats away to Dundee United, Hearts and Hibernian three years on the bounce in the Scottish Cup. When silverware was on the line the Dons folded like a pack of cards. A mortifying League Cup exit at the hands of Third Division amateurs Queen's Park in 2006 further highlighted Calderwood's issues with one-off cup clashes. The woes came to a head in 2008. Aberdeen had not reached the semi-final stage of the Scottish Cup for eight years – their worst run in the competition since 1977. That drought looked odds-on to be extended as the Dons were handed a tough quarter-final against Celtic, yet they were denied a famous win at Pittodrie as Celtic scored in the last minute to earn a replay back in Glasgow. It looked like the slim hopes of progression had been crushed, considering Celtic had already overcome reigning European champions AC Milan at Parkhead in the Champions League earlier that season. Aberdeen, it turned out, could do what the *Rossoneri* could not. The not-so-prolific Darren Mackie showed Kaká and co. how it was done, the striker grabbing the only goal of the replay to fire Calderwood's charges to Hampden for the first time since 2000.

The semi-final draw paired Aberdeen with First Division side Queen of the South – it was a golden opportunity to reach the final. Instead, it heralded a new era of Hampden heartache. The early warning signs that it was going to be anything but easy smacked Aberdeen in the face when Queen of the South took the lead after 20 minutes. However, fears were quickly lessened a quarter of an hour later with Andrew Considine equalising to send the sides in level at the break. Aberdeen had been disjointed, poor defensively and seemed intent on making their afternoon much more difficult than it ought to have been. After all, this was the same Aberdeen who had drawn 2-2 with Bayern Munich at Pittodrie just two months earlier.

If the Red Army thought that things could only improve, they were wrong. A crazy 15 minutes after the restart saw the goals rain in as Queen of the South went ahead again twice – Aberdeen pegging them back on both occasions. Just as Considine looked to have once again salvaged his side from embarrassment, epitomising the ludicrous nature of the game, former Aberdeen striker Steve Tosh scored immediately from the kick-off, heading up the other end and blasting the ball past Derek Soutar in goal. Inexplicably, it was 4-3 to Queens. Despite having the best part of half an hour to rescue the situation, Aberdeen failed to find a way through and crashed out of the competition. Given the significance of the occasion, it ranked among the worst results in the club's history – a list that had grown at an alarming rate over the past 15 years. It was one of the darkest days in which the once-great kings of the north were humbled by Queen of the South. By the time the Scottish Cup rolled around the following year, fans had just about worked up the courage to emerge from their hiding places. It wouldn't be long before they would be let down all over again; this time it was Dunfermline, another First Division side, who claimed a significant victory at Pittodrie. The heady days of the 1980s had never felt further away, the club a vestige of its former self.

What better way then to seek a return to the glory years than appointing one of the club's great legends as manager? With Jimmy Calderwood departing at the end of the 2008/09 season, the board approached Motherwell to lure Mark McGhee north. McGhee was the Dons' star striker during the Ferguson years, finding the back of the net 100 times, and was the man who had crossed the ball in to John Hewitt to score the most famous goal in the club's history. However, after McGhee's comments in his first press conference as Aberdeen boss, it wasn't exactly a hero's welcome that awaited. 'I have looked at [the Celtic] opportunity, I didn't get that job but I then moved on to come to Aberdeen quickly. The Celtic thing should not in any way undermine things – quite the opposite actually. Maybe Aberdeen fans should be thinking that they have a manager that was considered by Celtic,' he said, amid talk that he could have also taken the job at Parkhead. It didn't go down too well, and neither did the first result of his tenure: Aberdeen lost 5-1 at home to Czech outfit Sigma Olomouc in the third qualifying round of the Europa League, their worst European result, and it set the tone for McGhee's time in charge.

McGhee had won the Scottish Cup five times as a player, three of those in the red of Aberdeen, and he was desperate to do so as a manager. With the team struggling in the league, his hopes of a morale-boosting cup run looked to be his only route to getting the support back onside. A decent victory over Hearts at Pittodrie saw Aberdeen progress to the fifth round, where they were drawn away to Raith Rovers. A 90th-minute equaliser in that game spared the Dons' blushes to secure a replay back at Pittodrie where McGhee was confident of finishing the job. His belief was misplaced, the Dons turning in a terrible performance to crash out of the cup to lower-league opposition for the third successive year. The full-time whistle sparked a chorus of boos from dejected supporters, some even throwing scarves on to the pitch such was their disgust. They had seen enough. Twenty years had now passed since Aberdeen had lifted the trophy.

* * *

The following season, the Dons, now under the charge of Craig Brown, were comfortably beaten by Celtic at Hampden at the semi-final stage of both cup competitions. It was almost met with a sigh of relief from the supporters. There would be no cup shock, no embarrassment this year, at least. They wouldn't have to wait long for the misery to return. A defeat to part-time East Fife at Pittodrie in the League Cup the season after felt like rock bottom. Under 4,000 turned out to support the team that night in what was one of the lowest attendances ever recorded at Pittodrie. 'I would say that was arguably the worst result of my managerial career,' said Brown after the game. It was indicative of the deep-rooted apathy which had set in at the club. Aberdeen did actually make a return to the national stadium that season, facing off against Hibs in the Scottish Cup semi-final. Once again, it ended in disappointment – a late Leigh Griffiths goal sending the Red Army home with the now all-too-familiar feeling of failure. For those who had basked in the glory years the club's current plight was a bitter comedown. But there was also now an entire generation who had never known anything other than Scottish Cup suffering. It was as if the football gods were reclaiming their debt, now exacting years of pain and punishment in return for the riches they had once showered upon the Dons throughout the 80s.

With Scottish football undergoing a bit of a shake-up in the early 2010s, the fortunes of the Granite City's struggling club looked to be on the up following the arrival of Derek McInnes in 2013. McInnes brought the sweet taste of silverware back to Pittodrie at the first time of asking, winning the League Cup in his first season as manager. It was Aberdeen's first trophy in the cabinet for 19 years and the city was buzzing. In reality, the team should have secured a cup double that season. Aberdeen had done the hard part, knocking Celtic out on their own patch in Glasgow, before going down 2-1 to St Johnstone in the semi–final at Ibrox. It was a bitter pill to swallow considering they had been undefeated against Perth's Saints in all of the league meetings that season. They went on to defeat Dundee United in the final. Just as it had for all those who had come before him since 1990, the Scottish Cup proved elusive for McInnes – it wasn't for the want of trying.

The McInnes era at Pittodrie lasted eight years, and for the most part was a period marked by success and consistency. Even then, the closest Aberdeen came to reacquainting themselves with the famous old trophy was that fateful May day in 2017. But it wasn't to be and McInnes would depart having only ever reached one Scottish Cup Final as Aberdeen manager. In the years since the Dons had last lifted the trophy, seven clubs outside of the Old Firm had got their hands on its big silver ears. Even Hibs, who had been chastised for over a century for not having won the trophy since 1902, ended their drought in 2016. Aberdeen were now the only club from Scotland's traditional 'big six' who had not won the Scottish Cup in the 21st century.

Despite the missed opportunities for more trophies, the club had stabilised itself on and off the park during the McInnes years. While the team delivered consistent top-end finishes in the Premiership, reached the latter stages of the cup competitions, and qualified for Europe almost every season, the infrastructure being put in place behind the scenes was equally as important as silverware. The club entered a new debt-free era in 2015, while the £12m construction of the Cormack Park sports complex put an end to the ludicrous scenario of players training on local parks around the city. Dave Cormack took on the role as chairman after Stuart Milne relinquished control at the end of 2019, and the new majority owner set out his bold vision for the Dons to be one of UEFA's top 100 clubs. That was all well and good, but the fans, just as at any club, demanded success in the here and now – and they weren't getting it.

McInnes's time at Aberdeen came to an end in the early part of 2021. The product on the park nosedived during his last two years – the football was banal and the fans were unhappy, thus both parties agreed that it was time for a change. McInnes would later admit that even he hadn't enjoyed watching his team during those final seasons. Former player and academy graduate Stephen Glass was earmarked as his successor. 'The thing I want to put on the pitch is an attacking style,' said Glass after being unveiled as the club's new manager. It was one thing to say you wanted to adopt an exciting brand of football to win matches, but achieving it, as it turned out, was much more complex. Just 11 months on from his appointment, Glass was sacked following a poor 2-1 defeat away to Motherwell in the Scottish Cup. The players were jeered off the park by the supporters, a torrent of angry boos raining down on a broken-looking Glass as he traipsed off stage left. It was a sombre scene. Aberdeen were without a manager and out of the Scottish Cup once again.

For the fans, Scottish Cup exits had become an annual tradition. A bit like Easter – the exact date shifted from year to year – but somewhere between January and April, you could rely on the club bowing out. It was simply what they had done for the past 33 years. The only crumb of comfort to be taken was that at least defeats to lower-league opposition had been consigned to the past. Or so it seemed. When the draw was made for the fourth round of the Scottish Cup for the 2022/23 season, Aberdeen had been drawn to face Darvel. 'Sorry, who?' was the immediate reaction from most Dons fans when the name came out of the hat. Darvel, a small East Ayrshire town known for little other than birthing Sir Alexander Fleming and his discovery of penicillin, was home to the West of Scotland Football League champions – that is the sixth tier of Scottish football. Naturally, the TV cameras saw the appeal of Aberdeen, seven-time winners of the competition, heading down to Ayrshire to face a club whose regular league opponents featured the likes of Auchinleck Talbot, Largs Thistle and Cumnock Juniors. This was a far cry from the heady heights of the Premiership. Thus, the match was moved to the Monday night for the television spectacle.

Although it should not have even been a factor, Aberdeen were coming into the tie under a cloud. They were in abhorrent form, and manager Jim Goodwin was under immense pressure. After football fans across the globe had witnessed Lionel Messi lift the World Cup as Argentina captain in the winter of 2022, in Scotland, supporters longed for the return of 'real' football. The much-anticipated first match back for Aberdeen was a home fixture against Celtic. Goodwin had over a month to devise a game plan to thrill the returning Pittodrie punters. He decided that the best way to get something from the game was for Aberdeen to barely leave their own half. A late Celtic goal saw the Dons beaten 1-0, all the while conceding 33 shots to Aberdeen's two. 'It's difficult to make a case for [the game plan] now,' Goodwin admitted in the face of fans' anger. Rubbing salt into the wounds, three days later Aberdeen capitulated at home to Rangers, conceding in the 95th and 97th minutes to lose 3-2. It sent Goodwin and his team into a spiral, and ahead of the Scottish Cup tie with Darvel, Aberdeen lost 5-0 at Tynecastle, piling the pressure on the Irishman.

Despite the Dons' form, the result was viewed as a formality, with William Hill, the Scottish Cup's official sponsor, pricing Darvel at an astonishing 33/1 to win on the night. Joe Lewis, Ross McCrorie, Leighton Clarkson, Liam Scales and Duk were just some of the names in the starting 11 – it was a strong line-up. As the match got under way at Darvel's Recreation Park – the club had been determined to play the tie at home, rather than switch it to Kilmarnock's Rugby Park – the cold darkness loomed, and the bright lights overhead had Aberdeen firmly in the spotlight. And they crumbled. Unbelievably, after only 20 minutes, the junior side were ahead, a ricochet taking the ball past Joe Lewis in goal after some abject defending. Goodwin looked lost on the touchline. Given the setup of the ground, which was used to hosting sixth-tier football and not televised Scottish Cup matches, space was at a premium. Behind the dugouts sat chairman Dave Cormack, alongside some other members of the Aberdeen board, squeezed on to a wooden bench which sat in nothing more than a shed. As the TV cameras panned over to smug-looking Darvel manager Mick Kennedy in the technical area, it captured the glum faces of the Aberdeen hierarchy behind him. If you weren't of an Aberdeen persuasion, this was truly the magic of the cup. If you were, you wanted the winter night to swallow you up entirely.

Aberdeen never recovered – although they did have a goal unfairly ruled out for offside – and succumbed to what was undoubtedly the most embarrassing result in the club's history. Scottish football went into a frenzy – the result became a national humiliation. 'Darvel was such a low and the club became a laughing stock,' said Michael Grant, Scottish football correspondent for *The Times* and Aberdeen supporter. 'It was just unthinkable. I remember the day after the game, Aberdeen losing to Darvel was on the BBC national news. It was on the lunchtime, six o'clock and ten o'clock news. There's part of you going "oh fuck off!" but then the other part of me was saying "this shows that we are quite big". It was just a horror show.'

The despair that the likes of Stenhousemuir, Queen of the South and Raith Rovers had all plunged Aberdeen into over the years seemed totally insignificant in the face of the Darvel result. It was the cup shock to end all cup shocks. Until their day of salvation, Darvel was a burden that the Aberdeen supporters would need to bear. In deepest, darkest Ayrshire, the Dons, once the conquerors of the great Real Madrid at their zenith, had found their nadir.

3

Hampden Heartache

DESPERATE CUP defeats to lower-league opposition had come to define the now 35-year period in which Aberdeen had failed to lift the Scottish Cup. Before Jimmy Thelin arrived at the club in the summer of 2024, the Dons had featured in just three of the competition's finals since 1990. For a club of their stature, averaging almost one final a decade was nowhere near the levels expected by the fans or the club itself. For comparison, Hearts had managed seven, even lifting the trophy on three of those occasions. In truth, despite the length of time that had passed, Aberdeen had rarely even come close to welcoming the famous old trophy back into the Pittodrie cabinet; the closest shave with glory had been against an invincible Celtic side managed by Brendan Rodgers.

The Aberdeen squad of the 2016/17 season was a special group. The league campaign had been the best of the 21st century for the club, the Dons racking up a club-record 76 points, with some stunning results to remember along the way. They had blitzed Motherwell 7-2 at Pittodrie, Dundee 7-0 at Dens Park, and Partick Thistle 6-0 on the final day of the season. Graeme Shinnie, James Maddison, Kenny

McLean, Adam Rooney, Niall McGinn, Jonny Hayes and Ryan Christie were just some of the standout players involved in that free-flowing side that banged in an unbelievable 97 goals in all competitions – it was one of the top non-Old Firm teams of the last two decades.

The Dons, under the leadership of Derek McInnes, had finished second with their impressive points haul, nine ahead of Rangers, who had returned to the top tier for the first time since 2012. To back up their scintillating league form, they reached the League Cup Final – the club's first since lifting the trophy in 2014. An impressive flag display from the Aberdeen support, coupled with the bullish sentiment of their team lining up at the centre circle to face down Celtic's huddle, had the pre-match atmosphere bubbling. However, the act of defiance proved a facade for the apprehension lingering within. Aberdeen failed to lay a glove on their opponents throughout the 90 minutes, and Celtic, just as they had done in the previous two league meetings between the sides, swatted them aside with ease. Goals from Tom Rogic and James Forrest before half-time all but ended the contest, with a second-half penalty killing it off for good. 'Naturally, I'm disappointed,' said McInnes in the aftermath. 'There's a lot of pain and we're not feeling good about ourselves … It is important we pick ourselves up. I believe we can get back to another final this year in the Scottish Cup and I think we can use today's sobering experience to help us going into the next one.'

As the manager hoped, his team proved their resilience, refusing to let the disappointment derail their season, winning 16 of their remaining 22 league fixtures to secure a historic end to the league campaign. The excellent form extended to the Scottish Cup and, after edging past Hibs

3-2 in a frantic semi-final – in which Adam Rooney scored after 12 seconds – Aberdeen booked their place in their first final in 17 years.

The barrier to success and silverware for Aberdeen that year was a Celtic side managed by Brendan Rodgers. It was the Northern Irishman's first season in Scotland since making the move north after being sacked by Liverpool in 2015, and it appeared as if he was out to prove a point. They lifted the League Cup without conceding a goal and wrapped up the league in early April with eight games remaining – the earliest the title had been won in 88 years. The onus was on Aberdeen to find a way to beat this seemingly unstoppable team. 'They were brilliant – very hard to play against,' recalled Adam Rooney, who was in the thick of the contests against Celtic that season. 'We tried everything, different ways of setting up, different tactics, but Celtic always had an answer. Under Rodgers, they were well drilled, with a mix of everything you could want in a side. I remember one season we had Ryan Christie, possibly our best player at the time, and he couldn't even get into their starting XI when he went back – that showed the strength of their squad. We were unfortunate in a couple of other cup finals against them; they were just too strong, too good. We tried going man-for-man, we tried sitting deep, we tried having a go – but they always found a way through. Players like Tom Rogic were especially dangerous, capable of producing a moment of magic that could kill off an entire game plan.'

Although the challenge in front of McInnes and his players seemed a gargantuan one, they went into the final full of confidence. Despite losing 3-1 to Celtic at Pittodrie in the weeks leading up to the game, Aberdeen had bounced back and headed to Govan, claiming a 2-1 win to end a

26-year wait for an Ibrox victory. Impressively, the Dons rounded off the campaign with a 6-0 rout of Partick Thistle at Firhill. But it wasn't all rosy. During the final week of the season it had been leaked in the media that captain Ryan Jack had signed a pre-contract agreement with bitter rivals Rangers, something that came as a surprise to McInnes and didn't go down too well with the supporters. Having started on the bench against Partick Thistle, Jack was jeered by a section of the supporters when he was brought on to the pitch. McInnes would later admit to feeling hurt by Jack over his handling of the contract situation and had a decision to make ahead of the cup final. In a bold move, McInnes decided to strip Jack of the captaincy and hand the armband to Graeme Shinnie; it was a gamble that almost paid off.

'I remember not being very happy myself before the game,' admitted Rooney, who was told the day before that he would be starting on the bench. 'I had a feeling the day before, before the team was named, that the manager might go a different way. He'd been looking at a couple of options, and I'd just about got my head around the idea that I wouldn't be starting when it was confirmed. Obviously, I was disappointed – it's a cup final – you want to be playing. As a team we went into that game feeling good about ourselves, and it was more a case of, let's go all out and see what happens. After the disappointment of the previous final, we felt we had nothing to lose.'

The aggregate score over the previous five encounters between the sides that season had been 12-2 in Celtic's favour; however, after walking out on to the pitch to the backdrop of a stunning 'Stand Free' tifo by the Red Army, the Aberdeen players, despite the odds stacked against them, started to believe that this could be their day. That belief crystallised when Jonny Hayes smashed the ball into the net from a Niall McGinn corner after just nine minutes. It sent the fans into raptures, and, for a brief moment, it looked like they had found a chink in the invincible Celtic's armour. The lead would last for a mere two minutes, jubilation turning to dejection as Stuart Armstrong curled in a stunning effort past Joe Lewis. It was an instant response from Celtic, but the Dons refused to let the setback derail them. They regrouped and came on stronger, dominating the first half with the best of the chances. For the first time that season, Celtic found themselves in a genuine contest against a dogged and determined Aberdeen side, unwilling to play the role of a footnote in what many had already anointed as Celtic's day of destiny. 'Our attacking performance was really good that day,' said Rooney. 'We actually had a proper go at them. There was massive disappointment from the previous final, when we'd been beaten 3-0 and barely laid a glove on them. It's hard to get near them when they're full of confidence – the way they move the ball makes it difficult to even make a fist of it. But this time, the early goal gave us real belief.'

Aberdeen had done the hard part by staying in the game until half-time – all they needed was one more chance, one lucky break to take them back in front and dispel the myth around Celtic's invincibility on the biggest stage of all. That moment came ten minutes after the interval. Celtic captain Scott Brown swept a first-time ball towards Callum McGregor out wide, but it was just a shade too far behind him and McGregor had to scramble towards the touchline to keep it in play. He glanced up, seemingly ready to roll a simple pass back to his goalkeeper – but he stumbled. In a flash, Hayes pounced, stretching out a leg to cut out the ball. The ricochet bounced kindly into his path and suddenly he was racing towards goal, with only Brown covering for Celtic. Kenny McLean was thundering up in support, desperate to help out his team-mate. Two-on-one. Hayes tried to square it to McLean for what should have been a tap-in, but the pass was behind him. McLean stretched his leg out desperately but couldn't wrap his foot around it, the ball trickling harmlessly away. McLean collapsed face-first into the turf. Hayes turned away, head in hands. In the stands, thousands of Aberdeen fans stood frozen, hands glued to their heads in disbelief. It had all played out in slow motion – it felt as if Aberdeen's chance at lifting the Scottish Cup for the first time since 1990 had come and gone in that moment. The memory churns the stomach of any Aberdeen fan.

It was always going to be a tough ask for the men in red to maintain the intensity with which they had set about the first half, and so it proved as Celtic took an ever-tightening grip. Rodgers's side pressed and pressed, and a tiring Aberdeen threw their bodies in front of shots to stay alive in the game. The scrambling defence was constant, heroic and, crucially, unyielding. As the entirety of Hampden steeled itself for the first Scottish Cup Final to spill into extra time since 2006, Aberdeen hearts were shattered. Thunder and lightning had threatened over the darkening Hampden skies all afternoon, and, as Rogic received the ball in the middle of the pitch, the clock ticked into the 92nd minute and the sky lit up as a lightning bolt shot down from the Glasgow heavens. Rogic drove towards the Aberdeen penalty area, brushing off the attention of Anthony O'Connor, before skipping past Andy Considine just to the right of the six-yard box. With the angle tightening as Lewis rushed out to the ball, Rogic threaded a strike through the only gap available and into the back of the net. The east end of Hampden exploded as Rogic wheeled away in ecstasy.

'The fact that the goal came so late on was absolutely heartbreaking,' remembered Lewis. 'It had been backs to the wall for much of the second half, clinging on for dear life and just waiting to get to extra time for a breather. The plan was to regroup, maybe catch them on the counter, or at least see out the final moments and take it from there. But obviously, someone had other ideas. In the changing room, it was almost like shell shock – just pure devastation. The boys were absolutely knackered; they'd put their heart and soul into the game. Physically, they were shattered, and emotionally it was the same. It was a very difficult way to end the season, a real low point, and then you have to sit with that result for a while over the summer, which makes it even tougher.'

The dressing room scenes were mirrored in the Hampden stands by the devastated supporters. Their team had turned in a performance to be proud of, giving a Celtic side that had won all but four of their domestic games a real scare – they had come agonisingly close to creating one of the greatest cup shocks of all time. But it wasn't to be. Instead, the 2017 final became just the latest chapter in the club's long and painful estrangement from the Scottish Cup. It had now been 27 years since Aberdeen had lifted the trophy – after that final, more than ever, it felt like that wait would never end.

New captain Graeme Shinnie took to social media the following day to thank supporters for their unbending support. 'A massive thank you to all the fans who supported the team yesterday and to the city for getting right behind us all week! A horrible way to lose a final but we will be back hungrier than ever!' A man of his word, Shinnie's hunger for success at Aberdeen would never waver. In truth, he could never be satiated until he had lifted a trophy for his hometown club. The 2017 Scottish Cup Final was just the beginning of the story.

4

A New Don

THE APPOINTMENT of a new manager is something that arouses the senses among football fans. It heralds the beginning of a new era, allowing supporters to dream big despite all that has come before. Will this be the man to lead us back to the glory days? So often the answer is no, but fans don't let reality cloud their preconceived judgement that this is the one. A club finds itself in one of two positions when it is searching for a new manager. Either the previous incumbent has been ousted from their position after a poor run of results, or they have been poached by a bigger club with deeper pockets. Aberdeen found themselves very much in the former category. With the sudden and abrupt end to Neil Warnock's disastrous stint as interim manager, the Dons were in a perilous position. The old, reliable hands who had been called on to steady the ship had jumped overboard at the first sight of trouble – a relegation fight loomed, and the 75-year-old didn't seem to have the energy for it. After churning through five managers in three years, Warnock included, Aberdeen were in desperate need of a saviour. The club fired up a red SOS flare. From across the North Sea, a young Swedish upstart answered the Dons' call for aid.

Jimmy Thelin had been on the radar for over a year – he had interviewed for the job after Jim Goodwin had, quite literally, exited his post stage left. However, as caretaker manager at the beginning of 2023, Barry Robson stormed to eight wins from his opening ten matches, culminating in a 2-0 victory over Rangers at Pittodrie on 23 April. His on-the-job interview became impossible to ignore. Robson, who had rocketed the Dons into the driving seat for a lucrative third-placed finish, was eventually handed the position on a full-time basis, becoming the first Aberdeen manager to make the step up from the youth academy since club legend Willie Miller had in 1992. Although the board, led by chairman Dave Cormack, had been impressed by the up-and-coming Thelin, then head coach of Allsvenskan side Elfsborg, they had opted for a familiar face in Robson.

That's not to say that they said no and moved on. Any board worth their salt keeps a ready-made list of managers that they would be prepared to pursue should the need arise. Thelin's name was placed right at the top of that one-to-watch list. As if out to prove a point, Thelin returned to Sweden and oversaw a remarkable season, taking Elfsborg agonisingly close to their first league title since 2012, missing out only on goal difference. It was a season that transformed Thelin's prospects from those of a comfortable mid-table manager to a promising talent that could grow outside of Sweden. Clubs across Europe, including Sunderland and Swansea in the English Championship, became alerted to the Swede and began sounding out the possibility of luring him out of Scandinavia. Nine months on from Thelin's first interview at Pittodrie, Aberdeen were on the hunt for a new manager once again after the sacking of Robson, the team languishing eighth in the table. With Thelin still leading

Elfsborg and keen on new opportunities, Cormack knew he couldn't overlook him for a second time and decided he would move heaven and earth to get his man.

But who was this unknown quantity the board turned to in their hour of need? Thelin belongs to the school of modern-day managers who classify themselves as 'students of the game' rather than those who have enjoyed a distinguished playing career. Born in Jönköping, a historic trading centre in southern Sweden, in 1978, Thelin's playing career never amounted to anything more than featuring as a centre-back for his local club, IF Hagapojkarna. They never competed higher than the fifth tier during his time in their ranks from 1995 to 2003. Despite failing to forge a career as a professional footballer, what became clear early on was Thelin's passion and, more importantly, knowledge of the sport. His experience at Hagapojkarna convinced Thelin that he could do things in a better, more focused way. Having already hung up the playing boots and fuelled by the belief in their own methods, Thelin, at just 26 years old, along with his younger brothers Mikael and Tommy, took the plunge, boldly deciding to form their own club, FC Ljungarum, so that they could run things their own way. Naturally, Jimmy took on the onus as manager and immediately impressed in the role.

'After the first year in Ljungarum, many of us felt that [Jimmy] had made us very good,' Tommy Thelin told Swedish newspaper *Borås Tidning* back in 2023. 'At such a low level, with so little training time and so few resources. We had all become much, much better both technically and tactically. So, it is clear that we thought that if he can do that with us under those conditions – what can he do in ten years at an elite club?'

In his first season as a novice manager, Jimmy guided Llungarum to the sixth-division title, remaining unbeaten, winning 17 of their 18 matches and scoring 87 goals in the process. After four years he had taken the club to the fourth tier, a feat that didn't go unnoticed among Swedish football spheres. In 2009 he was approached by the top team in the region, Jönköping-Södra, where Tommy also plied his trade, about joining as an academy coach. It was an opportunity he couldn't turn down, and he initially coached the under-17 team. It was at Jönköping-Södra where Jimmy cut his teeth, getting exposure to a professional coaching setup for the first time. He quickly made an impression with his meticulous and ruminative approach to the game, rising through the J-Södra youth setup, culminating in him overseeing the under-21 squad. Mats Gren, a former Swedish international, was manager of the J-Södra first team at the time. 'Me and Jimmy used to spend hours speaking about the way football should be played and the philosophy of the game. He would like to study every detail and ask for advice. We both used to agree on the way football should be played, so there was a great connection between the youth setup and the first team.'

In those early days, Thelin became known for his studious nature, spending countless late nights studying videos of teams and matches from across the world. 'He impressed me with his dedication and the ideas he would come up with from watching other games,' said Gren. 'Jimmy was thinking about football 24/7, and the conversations we had were always extremely tactical and full of analysis. Even if it was slightly different from the normal way of doing things, Jimmy knew how he wanted his teams to play and exactly what to ask of his players. He is a great communicator and someone who got the most out of those he worked with in Jönköping.'

It was during his time with the J-Södra academy that Thelin was putting in the groundwork for his future coaching career. While completing his coaching badges with the Swedish Football Association, Thelin spent time at the youth academies of both Bayern Munich and FC Porto, where he met and picked the brains of Vítor Frade – the influential thinker whose methods helped shape José Mourinho's philosophy. In 2014, Gren moved on from J-Södra to take up a position as sporting director at IFK Göteborg and recommended to the club that Thelin take over. 'When I left the club, I knew they were looking to replace me with another coach from outside Jönköping. I met with the board and suggested that they would be making a big mistake if they didn't give Jimmy the job as we had such a good connection and his ideas about football were similar to mine. I explained that he would carry on the work that we had done over the last two years.' Thus, Gren can be credited with opening the first major door in Thelin's football career as the club took heed and appointed the 36-year-old in 2014.

What Gren failed to mention is that this unfolded just as the new Swedish league season was days away from kicking off. Thelin was approached by the club about filling the vacant position on the evening of Thursday, 2 April. By Saturday, he was picking the team to face off against GIF Sundsvall in the opening game of the Superettan, the Swedish second tier. It was very much a case of being thrown in the deep end, and after failing to win any of his opening four games, despite his steadfast self-belief, the young manager would have been doubting whether taking on the role had been the right decision. Things finally clicked for Thelin, though, and come October he and his players found themselves in contention for promotion after a run of eight games without defeat. It was a remarkable season from a team that had been completely unfancied, having finished 11th the year before. J-Södra eventually fell short of promotion, finishing fourth, but did manage their best league finish since 1976.

It was an impressive breakthrough season as head coach from Thelin, who had deployed a style of football designed to hurt the opposition as quickly as possible. 'We played a game based on having the ball within the team, but also that the closest route to the goal is the best,' explained Fredrich Fendrich, one of Thelin's trusted midfielders during his time at the club. 'On the pitch, he was very meticulous with details, how we should act in certain situations, for example. But at the same time, he also gave us space to solve situations on the pitch on our own with the help of his ideas. He took a lot of inspiration from other great coaches when we had video analysis, but as a person he was very convincing about his way of playing but respected that people could have opinions about certain parts of his style of play. From a personal perspective, his main qualities were getting a group together, giving responsibility to the players and giving confidence to the players both on and off the field. He made many people grow, including me. He was a passionate coach who gave everything for us players and the team right from the start.'

The positive atmosphere Thelin had created carried into the new campaign and his contemporary ideas revitalised a team that had long been accustomed to languishing in Sweden's lower divisions since its golden era of the late 1940s and 50s. A remarkable start to the season saw J-Södra win their opening five games, conceding just a single goal in the process. The impetus never subsided, and they stormed to the title, finishing one point ahead of Graham Potter's well-publicised Östersund side. Taking a provincial outfit like J-Södra to the Allsvenskan, Sweden's top tier, for the first time in 46 years was a feat that turned heads across the country. It was also a huge local achievement, considering that ice hockey, particularly the local team HV, holds far greater professional sporting prominence in Jönköping than football. The accomplishment, which had even been achieved with a large core of local players – including Thelin himself – successfully put the city on the football map. Ten years on from winning a sixth-tier title with his own start-up team, Thelin was headed to the pinnacle of Swedish football.

Two traits had come to define Thelin's management style – his obsession with detail and collaborative ethos to ensure that every player felt valued. 'Jimmy has become a bit of a half-vampire, he sits up half the night analysing his opponents,' said brother Tommy during the 2015 march to the title. Jimmy approached squad management holistically, valuing the contribution of all players, not just the starting 11. He redefined the role of substitutes, referring to them instead as 'decision makers', a reflection of their tactical importance. 'You could see how much having a good team spirit meant to Jimmy, even during his time with the youth teams,' said Mats Gren. 'I think that comes down to his personality and that he is also a very good and kind person away from football. He wants everyone to feel important and wants everyone to go on the journey together. For a football manager, having that togetherness is important and Jimmy does that very, very well.' None of this came at the expense of being seen as the man in charge. 'He still created a distance from the players and you could immediately feel that he was the boss, even though many knew him before he became manager,' said Fredrich Fendrich. 'Off the pitch, he brought respect from the first moment and a convincing leadership style where everyone was included.'

Although winning the title with a core of local players was impressive, it meant that the team lacked the experience and nous for a campaign in the top flight. As such, J-Södra found the step up to the Allsvenskan tougher than the enjoyable title-winning campaign – but they still defied the odds. With room to spare, the newly promoted side avoided relegation, finishing 12th and six points clear of the relegation play-off place. The young coach had rubbed shoulders with Sweden's elite and, despite managing a club with one of the lowest budgets in the division, had kept them competitive enough that they didn't look out of place. It was the first time since the 1952/53 season that J-Södra had retained their Allsvenskan status – it was arguably as impressive an achievement as winning the league the year before. However, for all of Thelin's abilities, it would only ever be a matter of time before J-Södra were left marooned towards the bottom of the table, such was the financial gulf that separated them from the rest of the clubs in the top tier, and two years after their promotion they were relegated via the play-offs.

Thelin had hit a glass ceiling with J-Södra – he had taken them as far as their standing within Swedish football would feasibly allow and there was nothing left to achieve. Recognising that he had reached the end of the road, after eight years at his hometown club, Thelin resigned at the end of the season, seeking to take the next step in his managerial career. At that time he was linked with multiple Swedish clubs, including IFK Göteborg, one of the clubs known as the 'big three' alongside Malmö and AIK. Mats Gren, by then sporting director at IFK, tried to reconnect with his protege and bring him to the club: 'I tried to bring Jimmy to IFK Göteborg after he took J-Södra to the Allsvenskan. I had that feeling about him that he would just do well with whatever team he takes on. However, he thought the step from a club like J-Södra to IFK Göteborg was too big for him. I thought that showed extreme maturity as a lot of young managers would jump at the chance to make a name for themself at a big club. Jimmy is a smart person, and he wanted to continue to develop his game before managing one of the bigger clubs in Sweden. He said no to me and joined Elfsborg.'

Thelin was announced as the new head coach of IF Elfsborg on a three-year deal in December 2017. Despite turning down a big job offer, joining Elfsborg was still a significant leap; he was leaving a club that averaged just 2,500 home supporters, moving to one of Sweden's most historic sides, capable of drawing crowds of over 11,000 for high-profile clashes with Malmö. Elfsborg had spent the vast majority of their history in the top tier and had most recently been crowned champions in 2012, so the expectation on Thelin as he took up his post as head coach was to deliver results. Things didn't go to plan in his first season at the Borås-based club, however. 'Everything in that first season for Jimmy Thelin was down,' explained Joel Besseling, a football journalist who covers Elfsborg for the *Gothenburg Post*. 'Elfsborg had been a club that was very well run, and they had established themself as the best club outside of the big cities since 2005. However, when Thelin arrived in late 2017, the club had blown a lot of the money they had collected from previous European campaigns. Thelin inherited a very old and slow squad that didn't fit his style of play, but he had very little money to spend to be able to change things. The club called for patience and the message from the board that this was going to be a project to get the club back challenging at the top of the table.'

Thelin's new side won just one of their opening seven matches. That culminated in a 5-0 hammering away to Häcken, after which the Elfsborg fans left their team in no doubt as to what they thought of the current situation, launching a tirade of abuse from the stands. A section of the ire was directed at the new manager, who many called on to be sacked. It was the worst possible start to the young Swede's first major job; however, those at the club were quick to rally round him. Club legend and 148-time Swedish cap Anders Svensson took to social media in defence of Thelin, who he rated highly: 'Reading and hearing all the so-called supporters' words about Jimmy Thelin in particular makes me both sad and angry. In my opinion, he is one of Sweden's most exciting coaches for the future. Elfsborg has had enormous success in the last ten years, but also an incredibly good generation that is now gone, and they are trying to build something new. I think we supporters should have a little self-awareness and support Jimmy and everyone who works around the clock to create something new and exciting in the club.'

Elfsborg finished 12th in Thelin's first season – their worst league finish since returning to the Allsvenskan in 1997. Things failed to improve at the beginning of the 2019 season, and the fans were becoming increasingly disenchanted with a year and a half of mediocre results. However, that summer was when things started to change.

'Thelin recognised that with the group of players he had, it wasn't working, and he needed to try something different,' said Joel Besseling. 'He made a brave change and mixed up the club's favoured possession-based football to one that relied more on counterattacking, high pressing and quick transitions. From mid-August, Elfsborg lost only one of their remaining 11 games, and had become one of the best teams in the league at playing counterattacking football. That's when the good times began for Elfsborg.'

The 2020 Allsvenskan season, like everywhere else across the globe, was heavily affected by the impact of the COVID-19 pandemic. Matches were forced to be played behind closed doors with no fans, meaning that trips to Malmö, AIK and IFK Göteborg lacked the same level of intimidation as they usually would with a strong raucous home support. In the absence of fans, matches took on a very tactical nature, something in which Thelin thrived. Carrying on the excellent form from the previous year, he oversaw a remarkable season in which Elfsborg lost only three games, the fewest in the league, and ended up in second behind Malmö. Thelin's Elfsborg became synonymous with quick, direct football and were a team that dominated the transition phases. Although they could not be there in person, the fans began to like what they were seeing.

As supporters returned in 2021, Elfsborg consolidated with a fourth-placed finish, and Thelin had now established himself as one of the country's hottest managerial prospects. Reporting on the daily ongoing events at the club, Besseling witnessed first-hand the impact he was having: 'Elfsborg is at heart a small club and is operated by a few people. Jimmy was essentially running the club in tandem with the club director, Stefan Andreasson, during his time there. Jimmy was developing the overall football strategy, the type of players they wanted to sign, how the youth teams should be developed, and even right down to the details of where the team would go on training camps. Off the pitch, he wanted a more disciplined team. In his final three years at Elfsborg, there were no players speaking out in the media – he kept the group tight and instilled a real sense of calm within the squad. There was never any drama under his management. He achieved that by taking real pride in making everyone feel involved, not just the starting 11. From what I gathered, speaking to the players, he put a lot of emphasis on team chemistry. Just before the 2023 season, they changed the rooming arrangements during a pre-season trip – mixed it all up – and it worked. The mood was really positive for most of Jimmy's time at the club. He also knew when to be serious or show anger – he picked his moments carefully, and the players respected that. His work ethic was incredible. He was in every day from 7am to 7pm, and the squad saw that. He didn't have an impressive playing career to lean on, but what he had was an insatiable work ethic. He worked his tail off for Elfsborg.'

Although stuttering to a mediocre sixth-placed finish in 2022, the club continued to lay the groundwork for what was to come. The 2023 Allsvenskan campaign would prove to be the tangible payoff of Thelin's methodical, all-consuming approach. The squad remained largely the same at the beginning of 2023, which allowed Thelin to work closely with the group of players he had, drilling into them his ideas. The year would see him perfect his fast-paced, counterattacking 4-2-3-1 formation, deploying it in over 90 per cent of matches to devastating effect. A disappointing 2-0 defeat at home to Häcken on the opening weekend seemed to spark a fire under Elfsborg that would burn bright for the remainder of the season. They pitched up at Kalmar on matchday 16 for a chance to go top of the league, solidifying their intent that they were genuine title challengers. Half an hour into the game, Elfsborg did what they had done so many times before: they launched a lightning-fast counterattack and Niklas Hult made it 1-0 in the blink of an eye. Hult was interviewed as he walked off the pitch by broadcaster discovery+. 'They have a lot of ball, and we know that. We like to counterattack; we are good at it. And the goal we scored is a prime example of that,' he said.

A helpless Kalmar could do nothing to stop the yellow-and-black blitz which ensued in the second half, and Elfsborg emerged 4-0 winners, taking them to the top of the table. There they would stay until the very last day of the season, where they headed to title rivals Malmö with a three-point cushion; all they had to do was avoid defeat to clinch their first league title in 11 years. They lost 1-0, no thanks to a second-half penalty, and saw the trophy slip from their grasp, painfully losing the title by a three-goal margin. It was a devastating end to what had been an incredible season for Thelin and Elfsborg. In a twist of sardonic fate, Thelin had amassed five more points than Elfsborg had garnered in their 2012 title tilt – it still wasn't enough. Despite the soul-crushing defeat at the final hurdle, Thelin, in a manner which had come to define the Swede, kept a cool head when speaking after the game. 'It was a very emotional end to a fantastic season,' he told *Borås Tidning* in the immediate aftermath. 'The players have put their souls into this and have achieved incredible feats. We have broken the club's points record, been stable over a long period of time, and won

20 out of 30 matches. It's tough now, but in a while I hope that all the players can feel proud of this season.'

Although missing out on the title, Thelin would not end the season empty-handed: recognised by the wider Swedish football community for the sensational season Thelin had overseen, he was deservedly voted as Swedish Football Manager of the Year. It was a scant reward for a man who placed immeasurable value in the essence of a team, preferring to shy away from the limelight. The Elfsborg board quickly moved to secure their man on a long-term deal. In truth, it was probably more about safeguarding their asset for the day a club would come calling on Thelin's services. 'After the 2023 season, Thelin signed up with some agents, as I think after six seasons he had decided in his head that he was ready to move on when the right opportunity came along,' explained Besseling. 'In the winter, there was a big job available in Sweden, the national team coach. I heard that he interviewed for the job with the federation and that he was interested; however, eventually, he decided that it wasn't the right time for him. Career-wise, he wanted something else and to continue in club football. At that time, he was linked with several moves away from Sweden, but nothing ever came of them.'

As Thelin prepared for his seventh season leading Elfsborg, a familiar opportunity, one that had previously caught his eye, reappeared. Aberdeen, Scotland's third-largest club, having just dismissed Barry Robson, were back in the market for a new manager, and this time chairman Dave Cormack got his man. Jimmy Thelin was announced as Aberdeen's 26th permanent manager, just the second from outside the British Isles, on 16 April 2024.

5

Jimmy's Invincibles

ALTHOUGH JIMMY Thelin was announced in mid-April, he wouldn't officially take up the post until 3 June – 48 days later. Under unusual circumstances, such was Thelin's loyalty to Elfsborg and their supporters, who he was now revered by, he continued on until a replacement was found. It would have been a frenetic period for the Swede as he essentially juggled two jobs – poring over the details of the squad he was inheriting at Aberdeen, while trying to ensure Elfsborg's optimal start to the new Allsvenskan season. His final game in charge of Elfsborg did not end in the way he had hoped – a disappointing 1-0 defeat away to IFK Göteborg. However, despite a bumpy run of results preceding his exit, the new Dons boss left for Scotland sound in the knowledge that he had smoothed over the transition to new coach Oscar Hiljemark.

Thelin, along with his right-hand men Emir Bajrami and Christer Persson, arrived in the Granite City in the middle of June, ready to get down to work. At his previous two clubs, Thelin had become known as a builder, creating a culture of stability, grounded in nurturing young talent and effective counterattacking football, over several years.

Aberdeen hadn't ended the season with the same manager who had started it since Derek McInnes in 2019/20, and even that was cut short by the COVID-19 pandemic. The constant upheaval year after year had taken its toll on both the club's coffers and the patience of the supporters. The board were ready to throw their long-term support behind the right manager. '[Thelin] has a reputation in Sweden as a team builder; someone who will methodically construct a winning side over time,' said chairman Dave Cormack in the statement announcing Thelin's arrival. 'From our point of view, we want this appointment to anchor the club for years to come, and to work with Jimmy and his coaching staff to create something special at Aberdeen. That will take time, we understand that.'

The promise of time, however, is something that isn't worth the paper it is written on in the world of football, and Thelin, more than anyone, will have been aware of the challenges awaiting him as he walked through the front door at Cormack Park on his first day in the job. First-team coach Peter Leven had kept the ship afloat between Neil Warnock's departure and Thelin's arrival. Until Leven's intervention, remaining unbeaten in the final nine games of the season, the threat of Aberdeen being dragged into a relegation play-off battle was very real. Severe question marks had continually been placed over the quality and, crucially, the mentality of the squad. The accusation levelled had been that when the going got tough, they wilted – it would be a trait the new manager would have to eliminate quickly. Leven had successfully overseen a turnaround in fortunes during his short spell in charge and was thus rewarded with a permanent place on Thelin's coaching staff.

Thelin might have only been in Scotland for a matter of days, but he had already been working hard behind the scenes ahead of his arrival with director of football at the time, Steven Gunn, and chief executive Alan Burrows. The first signings of his tenure were Irish central defender Gavin Molloy and Bulgarian international goalkeeper Dimitar Mitov. The acquisition of 27-year-old Mitov from St Johnstone felt like a statement of intent from the Dons, acquiring one of the league's top-performing players for a six-figure fee. Thelin was delighted: 'This is an important signing for us as Dimitar is a talented goalkeeper, coming into the prime of his career, and these types of players are vital to a successful squad.' Mitov, a commanding presence in the box and a fantastic shot-stopper, endeared himself to the Red Army immediately. 'As soon as I heard there was interest from Aberdeen I called my agent and said get it done,' were the Bulgarian's first words as an Aberdeen player. The signing would prove pivotal.

As the players returned for pre-season, Thelin was immediately met with his first significant challenge: forward Luís Lopes, known as Duk, had failed to report for the first day of training and showed no signs of returning as the squad prepared to jet off to Portugal for their pre-season camp. Duk, who did indeed fail to make the plane, had become Aberdeen's mercurial talent since arriving from Benfica B in the summer of 2022. The Lisbon-born attacker was initially viewed as an impact player during his first few months at the club under Jim Goodwin, utilised primarily off the bench when the Dons were hunting down a goal – which, during that period, was more often that not. However, he had quickly struck up a partnership with Bojan Miovski. Despite a turbulent campaign, in which Jim Goodwin lost his job, Duk netted 18 times, registering six assists to boot, and along with Miovski was the catalyst for the surge to third spot at the end of the season. With his ability to pull moments of magic out of thin air, as well as an easy-to-remember nickname, he established himself as something of a maverick among the fanbase. Clubs across Europe were alerted to the impressive numbers Duk had posted in his breakout year and were excited by his talent. The player, and crucially his agent, knew it too.

An indifferent second season followed, and by the time Thelin arrived at Pittodrie, the Cape Verde international decided to take matters into his own hands to force a move out. The club, unable to keep the situation under wraps for ever, announced that they were taking disciplinary action against Duk for being absent without permission. The situation was far from ideal for Thelin after only a matter of weeks in his post. With Miovski linked with a big-money move away, the manager found himself at risk of losing the two main goal threats the team possessed – contributing a combined 69 goals over the previous two years. Although a challenging situation, media-savvy Thelin had experienced something similar in his first season at Elfsborg. 'In his first year, there were older players speaking out in the media, complaining about playing time,' explained journalist Joel Besseling. 'He didn't like that and moved to ensure things were dealt with away from the spotlight. Thelin was very good at handling the media overall. The newspapers here in Sweden say that when Thelin arrives, you can send your headline makers on holiday – he doesn't give you anything to work with! He was always friendly, respectful and understood our job, but he wanted to create that tight team spirit that you can only do away from cameras and journalists.' Thelin's feet were barely under his new desk at Cormack Park, and already he was having to deploy everything he had learned during his six-year stint at Elfsborg.

The best thing Thelin could do to block out the noise was to win matches, and Aberdeen's season officially kicked off with a 3-0 away victory against Queen of the South in the League Cup group stage. Two goals from Slovenian striker Ester Sokler, coming either side of a rare Graeme Shinnie strike, got life under Thelin up and running. Speaking after the match, skipper Shinnie gave a glimpse into the determination of the new manager, alluding to the intensity Thelin had the players working at in a bid to stamp his style on to the squad. Premiership clubs, especially of Aberdeen's stature, are on a hiding to nothing when competing in the League Cup group stages, but Thelin guided the Dons through the opening four matches with ease, winning all four with an aggregate score of 15-1. In that time he had also secured the signature of his trusted former Elfsborg captain Sivert Nilsen on a three-year deal as he continued to shape his side ahead of the new league season.

Nilsen wouldn't take long to showcase his qualities in red. Aberdeen headed to Perth on a Monday night to commence their 2024/25 league campaign – the opening weekend of a new season being the latest ritual to fall victim to the commercial dismantling of the game we used to know and love. A first-half header from Nicky Devlin had the Dons, who were decked out in their all-new black-and-yellow away top, ahead at the break, and midway through the second half they added a second in silky fashion. Livewire Shayden Morris surged past two men on the halfway line before slipping the ball into Sokler, who had drifted into a pocket of space in front of the St Johnstone defence. Sokler instantly laid it off to Nilsen in the centre, and, with one perfectly weighted pass, he carved the Saints wide open, sending Jamie McGrath through on goal. The Irishman made no mistake, calmly guiding his finish into the bottom corner. It was an early glimpse of what Thelin's fast football was all about. The home team's late goal would prove to be nothing more than a consolation and Aberdeen picked up three points on the opening day of the season for the first time in three years. 'Good transitions are something we want to bring into our identity, and I think that is showing step by step, every game,' said Thelin after the match, pleased at seeing his work on the training ground coming to early fruition. 'Team transitions are what we want, not just one player, lots of players finding good combinations. I was happy with how they performed.'

Thelin's first league outing at Pittodrie was very much about out with the old and in with the new. Goals from Pape Habib Guèye, Jamie McGrath and Vicente Besuijen wrapped up a comfortable afternoon against St Mirren to ensure a perfect start to the Premiership season. Following the game, the club secured a record fee in the region of £6.8m for their North Macedonian striker Miovski, which gave the board the confidence they needed to immediately reinvest some of the cash for a new star man. Thelin's successful J-Södra and Elfsborg teams thrived on the electrifying pace of their wingers, consistently devastating opponents on the counterattack. He was keen to immediately bring some of that magic to Aberdeen and the board pulled out all of the stops to back their new manager; on 12 August it was announced that Finnish winger Topi Keskinen had penned a four-year deal. The Dons had splashed out £860,000 to pry the 21-year-old hot prospect from HJK Helsinki in Finland.

It represented the second-highest fee ever spent by Aberdeen, behind only the £1m paid for Paul Bernard in 1995. Just five days later, Keskinen came off the bench against Queen's Park and fired in a 92nd-minute winner on his debut to edge the Dons into the League Cup quarter-final. Assisted by Nilsen, Keskinen picked up the ball at the edge of the box, dragged it back to create the space on his left foot, and fizzed his shot into the top corner to send Pittodrie into raptures. The victory made it seven wins from seven games to start Thelin's tenure – the best start of any manager in the club's history – albeit five of those had come against lower-league opposition. The Nordic revolution was well under way at Pittodrie, and there were no signs of it slowing down.

The records continued to tumble; Guèye doubled up as Aberdeen swept aside Kilmarnock 2-0 at Pittodrie to make it eight wins in a row. It was a welcome return to the fold for the dancing Senegalese who had spent the first half of the year out on loan at Norwegian side Kristiansund BK. Guèye was given a standing ovation by the Pittodrie crowd as he made way for the club's latest signing, Scotland striker Kevin Nisbet, and it wouldn't take long for the new number nine to make his mark. The following week, Aberdeen headed up the A96 to Dingwall to take on a Ross County side that had just been dismantled at Ibrox the previous week. A frenetic game saw goals for both sides ruled out by VAR, while new stopper Dimitar Mitov saved a spot-kick from Staggies frontman Ronan Hale to keep the Dons on level terms – the big Bulgarian already proving a shrewd acquisition. With the game locked at 0-0, Nicky Devlin charged up the right wing in the 98th minute, passing the ball on to substitute Morris. The Englishman, known to the Aberdeen support as 'Shady Mo', skipped away from the close attention of his marker and cut the ball back into the box into the path of Nisbet. The striker's eyes lit up and he tucked the ball into the bottom corner for his first Aberdeen goal. The massive travelling Red Army, basking in the sun, flooded on to the pitch in disbelief as Nisbet wheeled away in celebration.

The dramatic last-gasp winner preserved Aberdeen's perfect start under their new manager and sent them top of the Premiership for the first time in almost a decade. Who then can blame the jubilant, bouncing Red Army behind the goal for rounding off the afternoon with the tongue-in-cheek chant of 'Fuck you Celtic, we're going to win the league'. Thelin, however, as would come to define his approach, was keeping his feet firmly on the ground. 'I'm really happy, but we need to stay humble,' he told the BBC's *Sportsound* after the rollercoaster victory. 'It was a tight game and Ross County were good. We can celebrate together today, but we have to keep working on Monday and focus on the next game.' The humble mantra which Thelin was eager to preach was more than just hollow words, but instead a belief on which he had built his career. When Thelin was awarded the season's first manager of the month award, thanks to his unbeaten start to life in Scotland, he requested that he be joined in the press photos with all of his fellow first-team staff members. 'Football is a collective sport and this award is for everyone that belongs to Aberdeen, the staff, the players who fight every match and every training session, and, of course, the supporters who back the team both home and away in such strong numbers,' he said, consciously aiming to replicate the successful team spirit he had cultivated at his previous two clubs, giving J-Södra and Elfsborg a stable platform for success.

With the Dons flying high, the dressing room was buzzing. In the background, conversations continued between the club and the absent Duk about his truant behaviour. At the beginning of September, with no concrete offers materialising from other clubs, the forward indicated that he would be keen to return, and following meetings with senior players Thelin agreed to welcome him back into the fold. Duk publicly apologised to the club, his team-mates and supporters. Thelin, with another attacking option added to his arsenal, had handled the entirety of the situation with equanimity. Had the team stumbled in the following games, there's little doubt critics would have pointed to the Duk saga and claimed it was a mistake to bring him back. That never transpired, however, and the red machine rolled on. A crowd of over 17,000 packed into Pittodrie for the visit of Motherwell following the first international break of the season. The teams were welcomed on to the pitch by a pre-match pyrotechnic display – representative of the buzz that had encapsulated the supporters with their team's stunning start. Another two goals from Guèye had the stadium bouncing as the Dons ran out 2-1 winners on the day. Thelin made it ten wins from ten and became the first Premiership manager to win all five of his first league games since Giovanni van Bronckhorst with Rangers in December 2021.

After yet another international break, Aberdeen breezed through the League Cup quarter-final with a 4-0 rout of The Spartans at Pittodrie, a performance Xerxes himself would have savoured, to set up a semi-final with Celtic at Hampden. Although rolling off victory after victory was no doubt delightful for Thelin, reaching Hampden marked the campaign's first major milestone. As fans revelled in the glory of their incredible start to the season, the doubters

---

were waiting in the wings for it all to fall apart. Some naysayers exclaimed that the fixtures had fallen kindly for Thelin and that he had yet to be properly tested. Aberdeen's response to those who doubted them was yet another win, this time on the road in Dundee, where first-half goals from a scintillating Topi Keskinen and Kevin Nisbet were enough in a 2-1 triumph. The sold-out away end was in full voice from first whistle to last, erupting with the now-iconic chant of 'Aberdeen, Olé Olé Olé' as both goals hit the net – and again in unison at full time. Had the team been tested yet? 'It is ridiculous to suggest Aberdeen are not being tested after the Dons made it 12 wins in a row at Dundee on Saturday,' wrote former Dons striker Duncan Shearer in his column in the *Press and Journal*. 'You could maybe say that after five or six wins on the spin – but 12 straight wins and equalling Martin O'Neill's 12-game winning start as Celtic manager in 2000? No chance.' Despite the defiant voices in the red corner, the critics were yet to be impressed. On to Hearts at Pittodrie it was, then.

Heart of Midlothian arrived in Aberdeen on 6 October 2024 in a terrible state. The Jambos, who had cruised to third place the season before, found themselves propping up the table, with no wins and only two points after their opening seven fixtures. The relegation form had resulted in manager Steven Naismith being ousted, so it was interim coach Liam Fox, once of Aberdeen, who led the team north to Pittodrie. Even before the two sides locked horns, Aberdeen had opened up an extraordinary 16-point gap on their visitors, having played a game fewer. May 2016 had been the previous time Hearts had left Pittodrie with all three points, and, as Keskinen's deflected effort found its way past Hearts' veteran stopper Craig Gordon after only two minutes, that certainly didn't look like changing anytime soon. Hearts recovered well, however, and looked the fresher of the two teams, despite a midweek trip to Azerbaijan in the UEFA Conference League. They got their reward just before half-time, levelling thanks to a header from a corner. Things got worse for the hosts, Aberdeen's perfect start coming under severe threat when Blair Spittal fired in a stunning strike from the edge of the box after 60 minutes to give the visitors the lead. Pittodrie was stunned into silence for the first time that season.

This felt like the first true test of Thelin's tenure, and he decided to roll the dice, welcoming Duk back on to the pitch for the first time since going AWOL. He had an instant impact. Positioned out wide, Duk surged past Hearts midfielder Jorge Grant, who immediately brought him down. By the time Grant got back to his feet the referee was waving a second yellow card in his face, followed by a red and pointing down the tunnel. Almost immediately, parity was restored as Nicky Devlin popped up in the box to volley home the equaliser with only 15 minutes remaining. The game had been turned on its head and the Dons were now odds-on favourites to push on for the win; they laid siege to the Hearts goal in a bid to preserve their 100 per cent record. On 88 minutes, Duk, looking every bit a man seeking to make amends, picked up the ball and drove towards the byline. His strength allowed him to shrug off the close attention of a defender and he cut the ball back into the box. There, waiting, was Croatian Ante Palaversa, who slammed it into the roof of the net before hurtling himself into the fans at the front of the Richard Donald Stand. A sold-out Pittodrie exploded; Thelin's Aberdeen had done it again. The sense that this team could do something special intensified tenfold in the aftermath. As fans poured out of Pittodrie, they did so studying the league table in disbelief. Aberdeen had opened up a five-point gap on Rangers and held stunning 16- and 19-point leads over Hibs and Hearts, respectively. Unbelievably, Aberdeen were now the only team across Europe's top 50 leagues to have won every game they had played that season. There was only one problem – Celtic kept winning too.

Some corners of Scottish football were still loath to give Aberdeen the credit they deserved for their 13-game winning streak. In the aftermath of the comeback against Hearts, one disgruntled Jambo took to social media to share his thoughts. His post read, 'Aberdeen aren't that good. They're just better at winning games than other teams.' Dons fans immediately jumped on it, with one even getting the exact words of the tweet printed on a T-shirt. The trivial back and forth pointed to the wider feeling at the time. Aberdeen were in dreamland and, despite the best efforts of opposition fans, refused to wake up. Even after that rousing fightback against Hearts, the suggestion was that they had been lucky. Next up for the Dons, though, was a trip to Celtic Park. It was mutually agreed then that should Thelin manage to get anything from a Celtic side who had replicated Aberdeen's perfect start to the domestic season, they could then be taken seriously.

If supporters were indeed dreaming with their team's remarkable start to the campaign, then they were jolted awake, sweating with how the first half panned out in Glasgow on 19 October. Celtic, as customary, dominated proceedings, and Aberdeen were heavily under the cosh. The floodgates opened in the 24th minute when Celtic's Japanese dynamo Reo Hatate swept home a first-time pass from compatriot Kyogo Furuhashi to put the league leaders ahead. Two minutes later, a defensive mix-up saw Furuhashi get on the scoresheet himself as he pounced on a loose ball in the box to double the hosts' advantage. Aberdeen, in the space of two minutes, had collapsed, their supposed title challenge in tatters – in that moment, it was mortifying that it had even been suggested as such, given the seeming chasm between the sides.

The Dons trudged in at half-time, fortunate that they were only two goals behind. The feel-good factor had evaporated in an instant, and it was a performance that fans had become all too familiar with in Glasgow. It was the biggest half-time team talk of Thelin's tenure to date. In the dressing room, the Swede told his squad to stay calm and refocus, reminding them that the same players who had won the last 13 games were the same ones sitting in the dressing room now. After a first half in which Aberdeen had been camped in their own box, Thelin decided to spring a surprise and take the game to Celtic. He made two changes, introducing Ester Sokler and Duk to replace Kevin Nisbet and Leighton Clarkson, who had both struggled, and suddenly things changed. Five minutes after the break, Sivert Nilsen scooped a ball into Jamie McGrath, who chested it down and threaded an exquisite pass behind the defence into the path of Sokler. The Slovenian timed his run to perfection, took one touch and rolled the ball past Kasper Schmeichel in the Celtic goal to halve the deficit. Sokler grabbed the ball from the back of the net and punched his arm in celebration towards the pocket of Aberdeen fans in the corner. Belief surged back through the Dons. Ten minutes later, Aberdeen broke forward again after a loose Daizen Maeda pass allowed Sokler to push up field. The ball eventually broke on the edge of the box to captain

Graeme Shinnie, whose effort took a wicked deflection, and Schmeichel could do nothing but sit and watch the ball fly into the net. Suddenly, from nowhere, Aberdeen were level at Celtic Park.

Incredibly, Thelin's charges thought they had completely turned the game around when they had the ball in the net once again ten minutes later. However, VAR intervened and deemed the ball had crossed the line illegally, via the arm of Duk. The red pretenders had shown their mettle when it mattered most in an enthralling contest. Some resolute defending was required to see the game out as Celtic assaulted the Aberdeen goal, but it ended all square. It was the first time Aberdeen had come back from two goals down in a domestic match since doing so against Kilmarnock in March 2020 – and they had managed it on the toughest stage of them all. The result had Scottish football finally sitting up and taking notice of Jimmy Thelin's side. Ultimately, Aberdeen remained behind the champions on goal difference, but they had turned up at their home and shown that they were more than capable of holding their own against Celtic. It was an echo from a time gone by. Willie Miller, a legend from that bygone era, had captained the team to dozens of victories in Glasgow and purred as he witnessed the Dons fight back. 'I've waited a long time to see this,' he said on *Sportsound*. 'It was on a knife-edge. I just thought it was refreshing – and you've got to give Jimmy Thelin and this Aberdeen team a huge amount of credit for coming down here and making a real toe-to-toe game of it.'

Aberdeen had passed the ultimate test, but the question quickly moved on to whether they could back it up, and a sold-out Pittodrie under the lights for the visit of Dundee United followed. The match, although dominated by the home side, looked destined for a stalemate as it headed into the final ten minutes. Chasing a goal, Thelin decided to replace Duk with striker Peter Ambrose, who up until that point had barely featured, totalling 81 minutes over six substitute appearances in the league. It was as if Midas himself had been reborn and now called himself Aberdeen manager. Within two minutes of coming on to the pitch, Ambrose broke the Tangerine resistance, bundling the ball into the net from six yards out. It was another Thelin masterclass; everything he touched turned to gold, and the Dons once again laid down the gauntlet to Celtic, going top of the league before the Hoops played the following day. Celtic, relentless, answered back by strolling to a 3-0 win over Motherwell in Lanarkshire.

As Aberdeen and Celtic exchanged blows at the top of the Premiership throughout the early stages of the 2024/25 season, the blue half of Glasgow was struggling to keep pace, and four days after dispatching Dundee United Aberdeen faced down their fierce rivals at an emotionally charged Pittodrie. Months of momentum, belief and determination seemed to converge in a single night as Thelin's side produced their boldest statement yet. The pre-match pyrotechnics were as electrifying as the Dons' performance; they dominated Rangers in the first half and could have been out of sight before half-time. Super-sub Shayden Morris lashed home with 15 minutes remaining, igniting an explosion of noise from the Red Army that reverberated all the way back over the North Sea to Thelin's homeland. The monumental win propelled Aberdeen nine points clear of Rangers, marking their most significant declaration of intent to date.

For a manager known for his composure, Thelin couldn't quite contain himself on the touchline, his self-composure briefly deserting him. After the match he remarked, 'It was an emotional game with a lot of things happening, and the fans were with us again. Of course, I enjoyed it a lot.' Aberdeen had taken 28 points from a possible 30. It was an unthinkable situation, given that from their first ten games in the previous season they had accumulated a paltry three victories. Thelin's team were the latest group of hopefuls from outside of Glasgow bidding to break the duopoly which had gripped Scottish football since 1985, and they looked like the real deal. However, as the manager kept reminding everyone, titles weren't won in October and, if the Dons were to have any chance of toppling an all-conquering Celtic, they would have to maintain this consistency for the next seven months. What followed from Aberdeen would prove to be even more unbelievable than what had come before – albeit for all of the wrong reasons.

6

A Barren Winter

AS ABERDEEN prepared to face off against Celtic in the League Cup semi-final at Hampden on 2 November, it was the archetypal unstoppable force versus the immovable object. After ten rounds of fixtures, the two were the only remaining unbeaten sides in the Premiership. Only two weeks prior, they had met in a frantic 2-2 encounter in the east end of Glasgow, seemingly establishing Jimmy Thelin's team as a serious threat to Brendan Rodgers and Celtic. As a result, many were predicting another tight affair at the national stadium between two teams who had been inseparable all season. That, even by the means of extra time or penalties, would have to change before the day was out.

For the first time in decades, sections of the Red Army were in a confident mood as they headed to Glasgow with their team preparing to go toe-to-toe with Scotland's reigning champions once more. The build-up to the game had BBC's Tom English comparing Aberdeen to Leicester City's miracle makers of the 2015/16 season in England, while Rodgers commended Aberdeen for their early season form. As a result of the impressive manner in which they had come through every test thus far, Thelin and his charges were being billed as the real deal. However, a cup semi-final at Hampden against this Celtic team was a step up from anything that had come before.

The momentum came to a shuddering halt and Aberdeen, for all of their pre-match plaudits, were dismantled 6-0 by a rampant, ruthless Celtic. The pretenders' challenge had been swatted aside with ease, and they had been placed firmly back in their box. It was clear Celtic had learned their lessons from the 2-2 draw and were out to prove a point that it was they who were Scotland's top dogs, and not Thelin's upstarts. The feel-good factor of the journey south had been shattered. Swathes of Dons fans stayed to applaud their team at the end of the game, a show of thanks for their stunning start to the season. For all of that, though, it was still another chastening experience in the south side of Glasgow for the Dons – another Hampden scar to sit alongside all the others.

It is no secret that Celtic hold all of the financial aces in Scottish football, a situation that has only become more exacerbated in the 21st century. In this modern football age, money buys you quality and a winning mentality. Therefore, did Aberdeen, despite their record start to a league season, truly believe they could go down to Glasgow and beat Celtic when it mattered? The Dons had been delighted in recovering from two goals down just a few weeks ago to steal a point against Celtic in their own backyard. A certain Alex Ferguson had been infuriated in his first trip to Glasgow as Aberdeen manager when his players skipped ecstatically off the Ibrox pitch after scoring late on to secure a 1-1 draw. He had been determined to rid Aberdeen of their inferiority complex against Rangers and Celtic. Forty years on from his departure, the club, no thanks to the financial imbalances now at play within modern football, was a faint trace of itself from those famous Fergie years. There was no doubt that the underdog mentality had seeped back in. In the immediate aftermath, Thelin naturally looked to move on from the scale of the defeat and focus on his team's response: 'The game is over, we are out. The most important thing for us now is how we act when we have setbacks, how we work tomorrow, how we prepare for the next game, how we keep the strength in our identity, and don't lose the belief. I believe that what we are doing at the core is still strong ... now we have to focus on the next game.'

Aberdeen's invincible start to the season might have been ended in devastating fashion, but they still had their unbeaten league record to maintain. The following Saturday, they hosted Dundee at home, and the supporters rallied, selling out Pittodrie for the fourth game in a row. The Dons rose from the canvas to lift the spirits of their fans, putting four goals past Dundee in a second-half onslaught, which extended their undefeated league run to 11 matches. It was the perfect tonic to alleviate the pain from the previous week. However, the faithful would need something much stronger to deal with what was to come.

Aberdeen's visits to St Mirren's SMISA Stadium since their 2018 Premiership return have been notoriously grim, yielding just two wins from a dozen matches as of November 2024, and, remarkably, no victories over a four-year period. Within the confines of the small, box-like arena, home fans conjure a vitriolic atmosphere that has turned matches against the Dons into intense struggles of will and determination, rather than that of a footballing contest. However, even taking those Paisley woes into account, Thelin's first trip to the town took on an even grimmer prospect as the country froze under a snow and ice storm in late November. Kick-off was delayed by an hour as St Mirren's staff worked tirelessly to clear the pitch of snow. Once the game did eventually get under way, Aberdeen were caught cold – a basic punt up the park from goalkeeper Ellery Balcombe allowed pacy striker Toyosi Olusanya to latch on to it and slot past Dimitar Mitov, much to the dismay of the Dons fans shivering behind the goal. The vibrancy and pizzazz that had exemplified Aberdeen's excellent start under Thelin was completely absent.

The Dons levelled in the second half, although in truth they never looked comfortable in the game, and a torrid afternoon in freezing temperatures was compounded as the home side scored late on to extend their own impressive unbeaten home record against the men in red to eight. Everyone of an Aberdeen persuasion knew that defeat in the league would come at some stage – but it didn't make it any easier to take now that it had. The fans who trudged back up the road could take warmth from the fact that while they had watched their team struggle in Paisley, Rangers had dropped points at home to Dundee United, while Hearts and Hibs remained 22 and 23 points adrift of them, respectively. What they weren't aware of, however, was that the same manager and players they had watched scale the domestic summit were now beginning the painful descent down the other side.

With Aberdeen's invincible aura broken, many were quick to suggest that their bottle had crashed. For those within the game who like to rely on data to fuel their opinions, the evidence also suggested that Aberdeen would be in for a tough few months. Expected goals (xG) is a phrase that will be met with rolling eyes and a dismissive wave of the hand when talking football down at your local pub. But for analyst departments at clubs up and down the country, xG is a clear and immediate indicator as to how a team is performing. Are they creating enough goalscoring opportunities? How many of those are good chances? How many are they conceding? Is this team more clinical in front of goal than another? Just as would be happening everywhere else, the Aberdeen analysts would have been monitoring the xG numbers as the season rolled on and, despite the euphoric feel-good factor engulfing the club, would have been concerned at what they were seeing. Even after the defeat to St Mirren, Aberdeen, according to xG data, found themselves a staggering 14 points ahead of where they were expected to be. For comparison, the next biggest outlier was Hibernian, who had nine points fewer than what the data expected of them. Despite sitting second in the Premiership, Aberdeen's underlying statistics painted a less flattering picture. They ranked sixth in net xG (expected goals minus expected goals against), indicating a significant over-performance relative to what the data predicted. This disparity was a clear concern for the backroom team, who no doubt feared that a statistical correction was inevitable. It was fitting then that Aberdeen headed to the capital just four days after their icy Paisley nightmare, as the two biggest outliers in the league went head to head at Easter Road.

Despite a bump in the road, Aberdeen travelled to Edinburgh in confident mood. Their opponents had experienced the antithesis of the Dons' early season fortunes and were sitting at the foot of the table with just one win from 13 matches. Before the match, it was being reported that should Hibs fail to obtain a positive result against the high-flying Dons, their board were poised to relieve rookie manager David Gray of his duties. The pressure was on.

Despite the converse positions of the teams in the table, the first half proved an even encounter and, on the 40-minute mark, Hibs took the lead thanks to a majorly deflected effort from their captain Joe Newell. As he had done so many times before, Thelin changed things tactically, bringing Shayden Morris off the bench just after the interval. The electric winger made an instant impact, driving towards the byline and getting the ball into the box before Jamie McGrath swept home to level. Aberdeen then hit the front when Nicky Devlin popped up in the box to scoop the ball over Jordan Smith in goal, and it looked for all the world as if the Dons had wrapped up the points – but the drama was only just getting started.

Nicky Cadden whipped in an unbelievable free kick to make it 2-2 in the 92nd minute, before Aberdeen responded in stunning fashion as Morris, pivotal once again, skipped past a defender and clipped the ball into Ester Sokler, whose overhead kick did enough to beat Smith. It was a stunning strike worthy of winning any game, but not this one. Almost directly from kick-off, the home team went up the other end and, with the last kick of the ball in the 95th minute, central defender Rocky Bushiri bundled it into the net to draw Hibs level for the second time in three minutes. It was a body blow to the Aberdeen players and supporters alike, who had celebrated wildly just moments earlier, thinking that they had won the game. Instead they had to settle for a point from a match that felt more like a defeat than anything else. Afterwards, Thelin showed his frustrations for the first time: 'There was so much emotion, and we lost concentration and made a collective mistake. That's a really tough learning point from us today – the game is not over until it's over, and Hibernian take this opportunity and we get one point.'

Under normal circumstances a draw at Easter Road was not a bad result, but this was a mentally fragile Hibernian on a run of eight games without a win and with their manager on the brink. The frenetic finish would prove to be a sliding doors moment for both clubs.

Aberdeen returned to the capital to take on the other half of Edinburgh later that week, leaving with a point once more in a hard-fought 1-1 draw. They might have only suffered one league defeat so far with their new man in charge; however, the seemingly unstoppable red runaway train had started to put the brakes on. In the space of little over a week Celtic found themselves four points clear of Aberdeen, with a game in hand. It already seemed like an unassailable lead for the Hoops, who were chasing down their 12th title in 13 seasons. Adding to Aberdeen's woes, the ever-reliable Mitov was sidelined for nearly two months as a result of a hamstring injury. It was a significant setback given that Mitov had been instrumental in the long unbeaten run. The Bulgarian goalkeeper had already saved two crucial penalties in games that Aberdeen had then gone on to win, while also boasting one of the league's top save percentages.

The nail in the coffin of any supposed title challenge from the north-east of Scotland was hammered in when Celtic travelled north on 4 December. A 1-0 win for the visitors, in a game severely lacking in quality, took them seven points clear at the summit, and still with a game fewer played. It was a jolt back to reality for supporters who had let themselves dream of breaking the Glasgow duopoly for the first time since 1985. In truth, with the resources Celtic control and with a squad over ten times the value of Aberdeen's, prising the league title north was always going to be a pipe dream. Thelin, however, had maintained his composed nature throughout the unbeaten run for valid reasons, often referring to the fact that the squad was still learning and growing with each passing week. Even he would have admitted the blistering start was unexpected for a team that had shown massive inconsistencies just the season before. 'For us, our journey is still a long-term one; it is not just about this moment,' wrote Thelin in his programme notes ahead of Aberdeen's Premiership fixture against St Johnstone at Pittodrie. 'We know that we have a lot of things to improve, and that's what we are trying to do every week in training and in games.' That game ended 1-1, as Aberdeen struggled to break down a dogged Saints.

Suddenly, with no wins in four, Rangers were breathing down the Dons' neck, and Thelin would have to rally his troops over a hectic winter period. Aberdeen rounded off the home games for the year as they welcomed Hibs, a month on from the compelling 3-3 draw. 'We have had a good start to the season so far, and it is important that we remember this at this moment when things are a little more difficult,' said Thelin in the matchday programme. 'Finally, I want to say thank you to everyone at the club, all of the fans and all of the people in the city who have made me so welcome since I came here in the summer.' By the time the day was out, that good start to the season seemed a distant memory as Hibs romped to a 3-1 victory, and from there the situation disintegrated rapidly. A Boxing Day battering at Rugby Park saw Aberdeen dismantled 4-0 by an aggressive, hungry Kilmarnock side who simply looked like they wanted it more. Thelin, his Christmas clearly ruined, was visibly raging as he did his post-match media rounds through gritted teeth, 'Our performance is not acceptable … You can win, draw and lose games, but not the way we did today. The effort we make for each other out there is not good enough. How we compete today can never, ever happen again.'

Three days later, backed by a sold-out away end at Tannadice, Aberdeen conceded a 94th-minute header to go down 1-0. Dundee United had exacted revenge for the Dons' own late show at Pittodrie the last time the sides had met. It was a sickener of a result, and the mood around the club darkened. Thelin would have been wondering if he had made the right decision to uproot himself from Sweden after all. Aberdeen were now winless in eight – a torrid run which had started with them level on points with Celtic and in a supposed title race – they now trailed the Hoops by 16 points. They were barely hanging on to the coat tails of Rangers, who they had been nine points ahead of after beating them at Pittodrie at the end of October. The frailties of the squad, which had been so evident in the previous season, had resurfaced. Defensively weak, outmuscled across the pitch, and struggling to find the back of the net; it was the worst possible combination.

The Dons, as many others do, stumbled, bleary-eyed, into the new year, where a home date with Ross County to open 2025 felt like the perfect opportunity to put the terrible run to bed and get back to winning ways. As so happens when things aren't going your way, even the impossible seems to happen. Aberdeen found as such with County scoring two unbelievable goals to snatch the three points in a game that was played amid a blizzard. At times you could barely see the pitch, and Aberdeen could see no way out of this hole they found themselves in, falling to their fourth defeat in a row. Results elsewhere saw them sink to fourth in the table, something which had been unthinkable just two months previously.

The January transfer window appeared to be the light at the end of this long, dark tunnel for Thelin. It would allow him to bring in some much-needed reinforcements to reinvigorate the squad and address some of its glaring afflictions, primarily the leaky and depleted defence. However, as deals were being worked on frantically in the background, the schedule offered no respite from the Dons' travails. A 2-0 defeat to Motherwell, in which Montenegrin defender Slobodan Rubežić was ordered off in the first half, had the manager despairing. Ahead of the next match with Hearts at Pittodrie, in the match programme he wrote, 'When the other side has some momentum, we are not strong enough to resist … Our mentality has to be better to deal with these setbacks. When things are hard like this, it's really important that you are strong and focus on the right things, and don't lose what you believe in, and try to understand the direction of the team you want to keep building.'

Earlier in the week, Aberdeen had made their first move in the transfer window, announcing the arrival of Latvia captain Kristers Tobers from Swiss Super League side Grasshopper Club of Zürich for a fee believed to be in the region of £600,000. The 24-year-old centre-back was thrown straight into the fray, and immediately looked like a solid acquisition as he helped steer the Dons to their first clean sheet since October – aided by a last-minute penalty save from backup goalkeeper Ross Doohan, deputising for the sidelined Mitov. Although the point stopped the rot of five straight defeats, it still meant Aberdeen hadn't won in 11 Premiership matches. Just as it looked as if a corner may have been turned, three straight defeats to Rangers, St Mirren, and then Hibs, with an aggregate score of 8-0, had major alarm bells ringing.

Thelin had made his start to life in the north-east look easy, recording victory after victory, and was treated as the club's saviour after a turbulent few years. It was assessed that chairman Dave Cormack had delivered a masterstroke and had found the hottest managerial prospect Europe had to offer, and brought him to Aberdeen. Now, in the midst of winter, nobody was quite so sure. A multitude of factors were contributing to the drop-off in form, the most obvious being that opposition managers and teams had worked out how to effectively nullify Aberdeen, which was to let them have the ball. Throughout the unbeaten run to open the season, they had over 60 per cent possession in only two of the matches. In the 14-game winless streak the Dons had over 60 per cent on seven occasions, the most damning of all being 74 per cent in the 3-0 home defeat to St Mirren. When confronted with a deep-lying defence and counterpressing, Aberdeen appeared utterly bereft of answers, often compounding their tactical ineptitude with egregious individual errors. It was hardly the formula for success, and the squad was shorn of all confidence and belief.

In the wake of the defeat to Hibs, supporters began to question Thelin's ability to motivate his team and offer up a Plan B, while the players took it in the neck for their 'weak' and 'cowardly' mentality. Former club captain Joe Lewis leapt to the defence of some of his old team-mates on social media. 'I'm not someone who usually gets into Twitter spats, but I did take issue with some people calling a few of the lads cowards,' said Lewis. 'As football players, you need to take the rough with the smooth. However, I think the assumption when teams aren't doing well is that the players don't care, the players aren't working hard enough, and the players aren't bothered. It's completely the opposite. The players care enormously, and it is their livelihoods that are on the line. When players are low on confidence, it comes out in many ways. Sometimes that looks like they're not really getting tight enough, making the right decisions, and that they don't believe in what they're doing. But that's all down to confidence. When you haven't got that real belief, you don't have the conviction in your movement and your actions, and it really can spiral. I think it's lazy just to say that the players don't care.'

Thelin had thanked Aberdeen supporters for welcoming him with open arms since his arrival, but the bright summer nights that heralded his arrival had now yielded to the long shadows of winter. The city would have felt like a very different place. 'When you play for Aberdeen, you live in Aberdeen and you can't escape the football,' explained Lewis. 'If you're doing well, it's great, everyone wants to speak to you about it, and when you're doing badly, everyone wants to speak to you about it as well. If you are in a tough patch, you can't wake up on Sunday, the morning after getting beat, and think, let's go out for a coffee, because you know you will get somebody saying something. It's difficult. Most people are great, but it's hard to escape it. The players during the spell under Thelin felt both extremes of that. They started the season as absolute superheroes, and then started to turn into the villains, and everyone is writing you off.'

There is no question that Thelin would have been concerned at the results, but he insisted that he had seen enough within those games to know that he and his squad would come out the other side. Withstanding difficult times was nothing new to the Swede, who had come through rough patches at his previous two clubs, one in which the Elfsborg supporters displayed banners asking for Thelin to resign. However, this time, the supporters were, in the main, firmly behind him. 'The fans have stuck with them through poor performances, which is unusual in football,' Willie Miller said on *Sportsound*. Thelin recognised this and knew that he needed to tap into it, once again taking to his pre-match programme column to get his message across: 'The togetherness we have here is a very big weapon for the football club and as long as we can maintain that, we will move in the right direction.' However, as well as the continued support of the fans, he needed new faces as he looked to put his own stamp on the team.

If the board harboured any reservations about Thelin continuing as manager then they certainly didn't show it, backing their man to the hilt in the January transfer window. In a bid to inject life back into their season, Aberdeen welcomed six new faces to Cormack Park over the course of January. Thelin reunited with his former winger and top scorer at Elfsborg, Jeppe Okkels, luring the Dane north from Preston North End on loan until the end of the season. Palestinian striker Oday Dabbagh was also brought in on loan from Belgian side Royal Charleroi to add another dimension to the frontline. However, the biggest area of supplementation was to the defence, with no more than three centre-backs putting pen to paper for the Dons. Kristers Tobers was joined by Tottenham Hotspur academy graduate Alfie Dorrington, while Dutchman Mats Knoester was picked up on a free transfer from Hungarian champions Ferencváros in what looked like a real coup. The Nordic influx continued as technically gifted right-back Alexander Jensen was purchased from Allsvenskan side IF Brommapojkarna for a reported fee of £650,000. Thanks to shrewd business and a bold, speculative transfer strategy that had brought in over £20m in player sales since 2015, Aberdeen had money to spend – and they had played their trump card. The wheels were now in motion, and there was no turning back. Thelin could only hope that in the second half of the season they would turn in their favour.

The Aberdeen fans unveil a stunning tifo of the city's coat of arms prior to kick-off.

The wall of red on the west side of Hampden.

Shayden Morris celebrates wildly with the Aberdeen fans after his cross was turned into the net by Kasper Schmeichel.

Ante Palaversa says he can't hear the Celtic fans after tucking away his penalty in the shoot-out.

Dimitar Mitov makes the crucial penalty save to win Aberdeen the cup.

The moment Aberdeen ended 35 years of hurt.

The Aberdeen players wildly celebrate after Dimitar Mitov's save.

Captain Graeme Shinnie lifts the trophy to end Aberdeen's 35-year wait for the Scottish Cup.

The entire Aberdeen squad and staff lift the trophy once more.

Jimmy Thelin, the man who masterminded the Dons to the trophy.

Graeme Shinnie shows what it means to finally lift a trophy for his hometown club.

Aberdeen chairman Dave Cormack celebrates his first trophy since taking over the role in 2019.

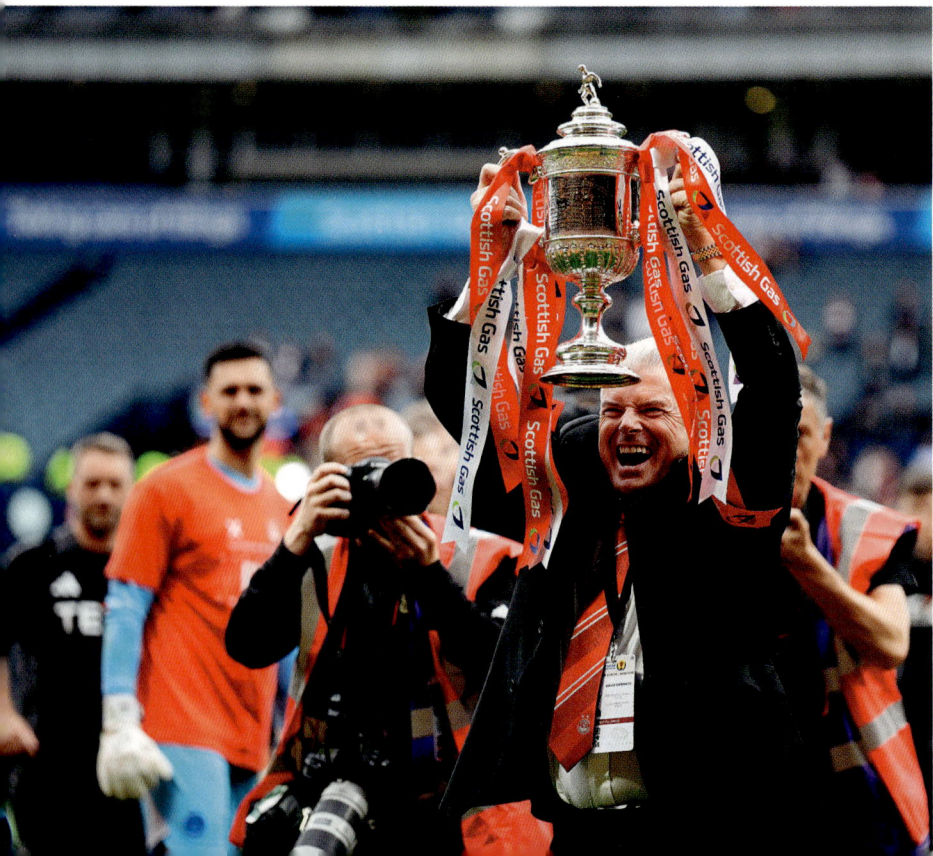

For once, the big screens at Hampden congratulate Aberdeen.

A hero's welcome awaited the Aberdeen players and coaching staff on their return to the Granite City.

Over 100,000 people lined the streets of Aberdeen for the victory parade to get a glimpse of the trophy.

An aerial view of the open-top bus arriving at the Town House, where the Scottish Cup party concluded.

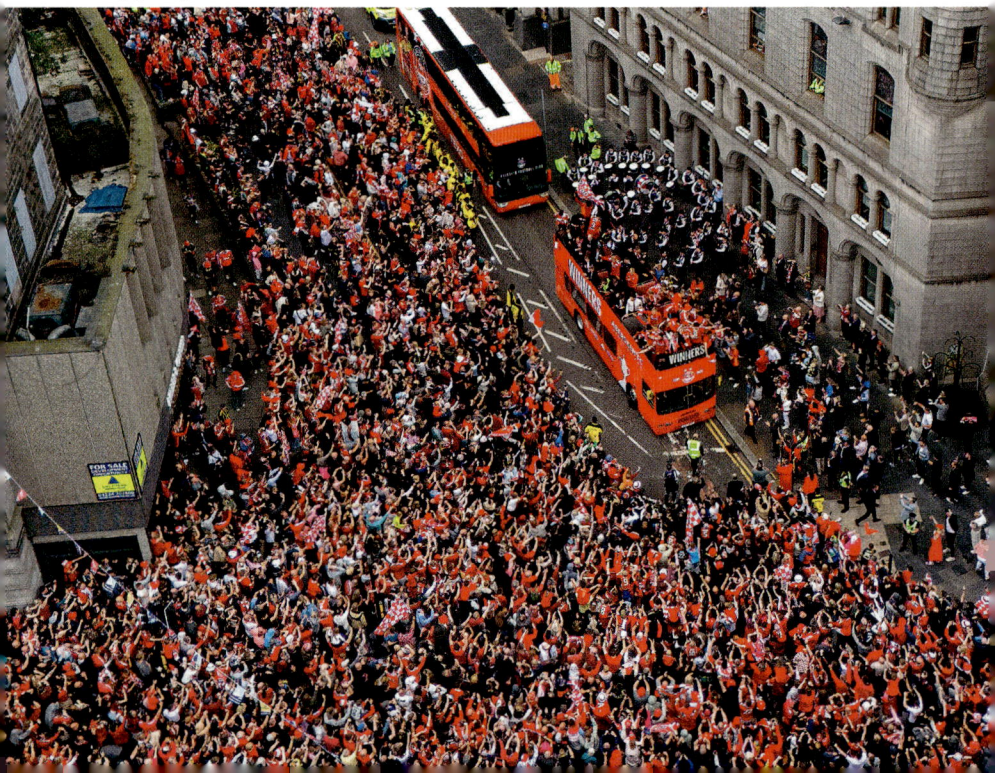

7

The Road to Hampden

WHEN THE draw was made for the fourth round of the 2024/25 Scottish Cup on 2 December, Aberdeen had lost just one of their opening 14 matches. It would be safe to say then, that when they were handed an away tie against League Two Elgin City, having avoided fellow Premiership opponents, the fans would have been rubbing their hands at the favourable draw. The closer the match came, however, with Aberdeen's disastrous form laid bare, the more nervous those in the red corner became about what now looked like a potential banana skin. While on paper a match-up with Elgin should have been straightforward for Jimmy Thelin's side, supporters remained cautious with their optimism. Defeats to lower-league opposition had come to define Aberdeen's relationship with the Scottish Cup since 1990, none more so than the humiliating Darvel shambles from only two years prior – the mental wounds that it inflicted were still fresh in the memory. For the fans, it felt like the next Scottish Cup disappointment was only ever just around the corner. And Elgin, who had only lost once at home in the league all season, were relishing the chance to show that they could go toe-to-toe with Premiership opponents.

Former Hearts manager Steven Naismith, who had helped carry out the draw live on BBC Scotland, had picked Elgin versus Aberdeen as one of the ties of the round, as, in his opinion, the two clubs were rivals. It was just the latest example of the common lack of understanding of the north-east of Scotland from those in the west of the country. The game did carry an extra bit of weight to it, but not in the way Naismith suggested – it was quite the opposite. Elgin manager Allan Hale was a lifelong Aberdeen supporter and couldn't wait to welcome his heroes to Borough Briggs in what would be a special occasion for the Moray-based club. 'I said I was hoping for a draw that would bring some excitement to the town and that's exactly what it's produced,' Hale told Grampian Online after the draw had been made. 'We are one of the fortunate ones to get the dream tie if you like. Being selfish, being an Aberdeen fan, I would have loved the experience of walking down the touchline at Pittodrie one time. But nonetheless to get them at Elgin and what should surely be a full house … it certainly whets the appetite.'

Thelin was a bit more coy about the tie, hoping not to draw too much attention on to his players, who had now gone 12 games without a win. Aberdeen's club-record winless streak was 15, and a victory in Elgin was necessary to ensure that figure remained untouched. However, it would be the Swede's first taste of the Scottish Cup, something he was looking forward to, and it was evident that he already understood the magnitude of the competition. 'The Scottish Cup, you hear it in the name, it is a really big cup and it's so important for everybody in the club and the supporters,' said Thelin in his pre-match press conference. 'For me, the cup here and in Sweden is so amazing because you can play these games against teams from different levels, and that is the core of football. You can create dreams, the passion. That is why the cup is an amazing thing.'

As expected, the tie was an instant sell-out, creating a buzz around the town in the weeks leading up to the game. As Elgin geared up for the clash, someone had even gone to the effort of selling half-and-half scarves on the high street. They weren't exactly flying off the shelves, though, with just three sold on one of the days earlier in the week. The sales no doubt picked up the closer the game got. When the Saturday rolled around, almost 4,500 supporters, 1,800 of those in red, packed into the most northerly football league stadium in Britain. A trip to Borough Briggs was, as Thelin described it, a journey back to 'the core of football'. Untouched in almost 60 years, it is one of those grounds that stands as a relic of the past, retaining the nostalgic charm that has long been lost in modern stadiums further up the pyramid – you even get to hand a physical ticket over to a real person to swivel you through the turnstile. The Aberdeen support, crammed into the west side of the ground, didn't even have to wait until kick-off to be disappointed as they quickly learned that there were no pies on offer from the stadium kiosks – it felt as if the suffering of this luckless run would never end.

As the teams were announced, it was revealed, as expected, that Thelin had shuffled the pack. The much-maligned Peter Ambrose was in from the off to lead the line, while Shayden Morris, so often the supersub, was given the opportunity to show what he could do with a starting berth. New signings Kristers Tobers and Alexander Jensen were also in, alongside Dante Polvara, who had just returned from a horrendous hamstring injury that had sidelined him for the entire first half of the season. As if foretelling a turn in fortunes for the away side, the winter sun bathed the afternoon in light, its low angle in the sky stretching long shadows across the pitch. However, the opening 20 minutes suggested otherwise as it was Elgin who looked to make a fast start and put a mentally fragile Aberdeen under some early pressure. Elgin's top-knotted number nine Dajon Golding looked like he was going to live up to the billing that his hairstyle evinced. A drag-back to the edge of the box found team-mate Lewis Hyde, who fired inches wide of the post inside the opening five minutes. Shortly after, a loose pass in the middle of the park from Polvara allowed Golding to latch on to the ball and drive at the Aberdeen backline. A floated ball to the back post found Ryan Sargent but he couldn't pick out a black-and-white shirt, allowing Sivert Nilsen to boot the ball clear to give the Dons some time to regroup.

At the other end Ambrose inexplicably headed over the bar after a neat cross from Jensen. However, it wouldn't matter too much as just over a minute later Aberdeen went ahead. Jensen, after skipping away from an Elgin defender on the left, poked the ball into Duk, who got his head up at the edge of the box and cut the ball back to Shayden Morris. The Englishman made no mistake and slammed the ball past goalkeeper Aidan Glavin. The goal settled Aberdeen and, in truth, the result never looked in doubt thereafter. A strong start to the second half saw the Dons dominate the ball, and Morris could have had a hat-trick if it weren't for the post and spree of saves by Glavin. It was all about Duk after that. The attacker, who had been welcomed back into the squad by Thelin after going AWOL in the summer, repaid his manager's faith in him. In the 72nd minute he rose highest from a corner and got just enough power into his downward header to take it over the line, much to the protestations of the Elgin players, who were adamant that Glavin had done enough to make the stop. The referee and linesman disagreed, and Aberdeen were 2-0 up. Elgin went down to ten men just minutes later when Duk was pulled back while charging up field, Lyall Booth receiving a second yellow card. Duk, involved again, found time to squeeze in one last opportunity in the 92nd minute, steering the ball into the far corner with a first-time strike to cap off a comfortable second half for Aberdeen. The long, winless streak finally ended, the players took the acclaim of the Red Army, who had continued to back them every step of the way. Helping the Dons into the fifth round of the Scottish Cup would prove to be Duk's parting gift as he would depart for Spanish side CD Leganés in a deadline-day move just a few weeks later, to bring the curtain down on his saga.

Aberdeen: *Doohan, Devlin, Rubezic, Tobers, Jensen, Nilsen, Palaversa, Morris, Polvara, Duk, Ambrose*
Subs used: *Shinnie, Clarkson, Guèye, Nisbet*

Elgin City: *Glavin, Cairns, Girvan, Cameron, Booth, Hyde, Gallagher, Leslie, Dingwall, Golding, Sargent*
Subs used: *Gavin, McDonald, MacDonald*

Despite that victory alleviating some of the pressure on the team, the reprieve wouldn't last long. A galling 3-0 home defeat to St Mirren immediately followed before an insipid display at Easter Road saw the Dons go down 2-0; after 14 Premiership games without victory they found themselves in fourth spot, and Hibs were rocketing up the table – the Leith side now only two points further back after an impressive run of their own. It was an unthinkable scenario considering the gap between the two clubs had been 26 points in the live table when Ester Sokler thumped his overhead kick into the net back in November. Things continued to be a slog for Thelin and his players in the league, but, just as the Elgin game had done, the home Scottish Cup fifth round home tie against Dunfermline Athletic came just at the right time.

In the week leading up to the match, the club had been working hard behind the scenes to get international clearance for new signings Mats Knoester and Oday Dabbagh to be able to feature. Striker Dabbagh would have to wait to make his debut; however, Dutchman Knoester got the all-clear, adding some much-needed freshness to the defence. Despite the desperate league form, one thing that wasn't lost on Thelin was the importance of the cup competitions to the supporters. 'There's no trophy for third place, but there is for the Scottish Cup showpiece final, the biggest game of the season here in Scotland at the end of the year,' he told the *Daily Record*. 'I've seen the footage, a lot of the scenes on Union Street the last time Aberdeen won a cup. That hasn't happened now for 11 years as we have to try to end that. You can't carry everything that went before – you have to create a new future to write our own history. It's a big club, there's a lot of passion with a good support, who have high ambitions.' Thelin may have understood the gravitas of the Scottish Cup, but winning it and ending Aberdeen's 35-year drought for the trophy, with the team's current form, felt a little far-fetched.

Dunfermline themselves went into the encounter under a cloud. Although recently appointed manager Michael Tidser had won his first match in charge, they were in the thick of a Championship relegation dogfight and were on a run of only two wins in seven. Consequently, even though media outlets were questioning Thelin's future, with some speculating he couldn't withstand a surprising cup loss to Dunfermline, the Dons' challenge was not as intimidating as anticipated. With the red tape successfully manoeuvred, Thelin named Knoester in the starting line-up, alongside two of the other January defensive signings, Tobers, and Jensen starting at his natural right-back position for the first time. It was a new-look defence but it made an immediate impression. However, the initial moments of the game highlighted the Dons' struggles, particularly their inability to find the net, with only one goal in their previous eight league matches. Aberdeen carved out several promising openings throughout the opening period, only for them to unravel through slack passing and poor decision-making in the final third.

Given Aberdeen's recent misfortunes, it almost felt inevitable that the visitors would punish the hosts' sluggishness with a sucker punch at the other end. Yet the blow never came. Instead, with half-time looming and the scoreline still blank, Pape Guèye – making his return after a long injury lay-off – climbed above the pack at a corner and powered Aberdeen into the lead. Five minutes after the interval, Jensen, pushing high up the pitch, drove a low shot from the edge of the box and into the net to grab his first goal in red. Although now two to the good, Kevin Nisbet somehow failed to extend the lead as he prodded the ball on to the post rather than into the gaping goal after rounding the keeper. It was a miss of the season contender and, with the way the recent run had gone, many concerned faces inside the ground worried whether it would be the catalyst for a Dunfermline fightback. Those fears looked to be warranted when the Pars were awarded a penalty just three minutes later, only for VAR to intervene as the foul was deemed to be outside of the box. The game could have veered in a different direction if they had pulled one back, but instead Nisbet made amends for his earlier howler and converted Morris's cut back to round off the scoring at 3-0 to send Aberdeen into the last eight. As the TV cameras panned on to the striker, he could be seen mouthing 'thank fuck' – you can guarantee the rest of the stadium felt the same.

Thelin, speaking in his post-match press conference, was delighted with the afternoon's result. 'We're now looking forward to the draw. It was an important game for us. We had to win. The players in the first half showed more directness. With how we arrived in the box and how we attacked, which was good, we saw some clear signs of what we want in the future and going back to this attacking approach of the game.' For all of Thelin's delight with his forwards being able to find the back of the net, the bedrock of the result was built from the solid backline, which never looked troubled throughout the 90 minutes. There would be tougher tests to come than a struggling Championship side, but it was a fantastic first impression from 26-year-old Knoester, while Jensen was a standout at right-back.

> **Aberdeen:** Doohan, Jensen, Tobers, Knoester, MacKenzie, Nilsen, Palaversa, Keskinen, Guèye, Okkels, Nisbet
> **Subs used:** Morris, Shinnie, Dorrington, Ambrose, Clarkson
>
> **Dunfermline Athletic:** Oluwayemi, Comrie, Mullen, Benedictus, Chalmers, Hamilton, Otoo, McCann, Wotherspoon, Stevens, Kane
> **Subs used:** Yeboah, Ngwenya, Ritchie-Hosler, O'Halloran, Hampson

The eight teams in the quarter-final draw were Aberdeen, Celtic, Dundee, Heart of Midlothian, Hibernian, Livingston, St Johnstone, and Queen's Park. The glaring omission was that of Rangers, who had been unceremoniously dumped out by Queen's Park at Ibrox in the round previous. Although struggling under Belgian manager Philippe Clement, Rangers had at least reached the semi-final stage in the last three years, and were expected to do so again. However, after failing to convert a last-minute penalty, they had been vanquished by Championship Queen's Park in one of the competition's greatest shocks, leaving the door open for another team to make their mark at Hampden. Despite their fifth-round heroics, the Spiders were the lowest-ranked team in the competition, and, with respect, were who every one of the other seven remaining clubs would have quietly wished to have been paired with for their quarter-final. It was Aberdeen who benefited and they would welcome Queen's Park, managed by former St Johnstone manager Callum Davidson, to Pittodrie for the second time that season.

Unlike the previous two rounds, Aberdeen went into the game with a decent string of results behind them. They had backed up their impressive victory over Dunfermline by posting their first league win in 15 matches, away to Dundee, to end their torrid winless run. Remarkably, the three points lifted Aberdeen back up into third spot despite having not won for the best part of three and a half months.

Suddenly, some semblance of confidence flowed back into the team, and they made it three wins on the bounce after January signing Oday Dabbagh netted in the 90th minute against Kilmarnock to snatch it 1-0.

However, just when it looked like Aberdeen were beginning to find their rhythm once more, another daunting trip to Glasgow to face Celtic awaited. The eventual 5-1 scoreline did not reflect it, but Aberdeen gave a good account of themselves in the opening 45 minutes and really should have been a couple of goals to the good after missing some gilt-edged opportunities. Celtic did what they do best and punished the Dons for their profligacy. The result was a far cry from the start of the season, where Aberdeen had been the ones to punish the hosts for their slackness, fighting back from 2-0 down to come away with a point and stay level on points with Celtic at the top of the table. The fortunes of both teams since had somewhat differed, with that February victory taking Celtic a startling 31 points ahead of Aberdeen. Despite the setback, Thelin's team looked like they had turned a corner. The following week they proved that their mentality was not as fragile as had been levelled at them throughout the winless run, coming back from two goals down against Dundee United at Pittodrie to claim a point in a 2-2 draw. There were still major question marks over the quality and durability of the Aberdeen squad, but finally it seemed as if Thelin had navigated his side out of the choppy waters which had, for so long, threatened to sink them.

It would take much more than a cup victory over lower-league opposition to reinstate the feel-good factor that had engulfed the club at the start of the season. However, a Sunday lunchtime goals show against Queen's Park had the ship reset on the correct course. Nisbet got the scoring under way when he flicked in a stunning near-post finish from Ante Palaversa's corner to grab his tenth of the season. Just under two minutes later, the lead was doubled as Shayden Morris picked the ball up at the edge of the box and drilled a low cross into the path of Dabbagh, who turned the ball home with ease. It was a dominant first-half display from the Reds, who ended the tie as a contest on the stroke of half-time. Another Palaversa corner drifted over everyone crowded in the box and dropped to Shinnie, who found himself in acres of space. The captain's first-time strike dipped and swerved and found the bottom corner of the net, dumbfounding the Queen's Park goalkeeper. It was a special moment for the 33-year-old as he marked his 600th career appearance with a Scottish Cup goal to send his side well on their way into the semi-finals.

Morris and Dabbagh linked up again soon after the restart, the winger's blistering pace once more opening up space before he squared for the striker to tap home Aberdeen's fourth with just 52 minutes played. It marked Morris's 11th assist of the campaign, confirmation that he had become one of the team's most potent attacking outlets – a notion that would have seemed unthinkable only a year earlier; back in February 2024 his Aberdeen career looked finished. Substituted before half-time in a bruising home encounter with Motherwell, Morris had been thrust into an unfamiliar wing-back role by Neil Warnock and endured a nightmare evening. He was culpable in all three goals conceded inside the opening half an hour – even giving away a penalty – before being withdrawn. That early exit proved to be his last appearance of the season, and it felt as though the curtain had already fallen on his time at the club. Fast forward a year and Morris was the terror of defences across the country, having reinvented himself under Thelin's mentorship. There remained question marks over his ability to impact games from the start, being preferred as an impact substitute, but 'Shady Mo' had established himself as an important player in the squad. His redemption arc was in full swing.

With the match over as a contest, Aberdeen took their foot off the accelerator and a consolation goal from Queen's Park failed to mask the dominant display that the Dons had produced, firmly stamping their place in the semi-finals of the Scottish Cup for the second year running.

Aberdeen: *Mitov, Shinnie, Knoester, Dorrington, Jensen, Palaversa, Clarkson, Keskinen, Nisbet, Morris, Dabbagh*
Subs used: *Ambrose, Guèye, Boyd, Milne, Polvara*

Queens Park: *Ferrie, Devine, Tizzard, Ujdur, Machin, Longridge, Welsh, Turner, Jurst, Drozed, Rudden*
Subs used: *Raymond, Hickey-Fugaccia, Hinds, MacGregor, McGinley*

The Aberdeen faithful breathed a collective sigh of relief when the semi-final draw spared them a clash with Celtic, instead pitting them against a Hearts side who were still very much struggling in the bottom half of the table. The players and management would never admit to it, however, but their reaction would have been similar to that of their supporters. The Dons may not have returned to their early season swagger but the team was in a much healthier place than it had been. The last thing Thelin needed ahead of a crucial run-in towards the end of the season, in the battle for third spot, was another battering of the confidence by Celtic at Hampden. However, taking on Hearts, despite their troubles, would be no easy task, and for both sets of fans there were some scores to settle.

The advent of guaranteed European football for the Scottish Cup winners from 2022 onwards had, in essence, created another prize to play for in the top flight. Thanks to the nation's improved UEFA coefficient ranking in the early 2020s, the Scottish Cup winners gained a more advantageous starting position on the UEFA access lists, directly entering the Europa League play-off round. Entering at this stage, at the very least, guarantees participation in a UEFA competition beyond the summer qualification rounds. Furthermore, if the Scottish Cup winner had also finished in the top two of the Premiership, thereby qualifying for the Champions League, then the Europa League play-off spot was awarded to the third-placed team in the league. Given Celtic's consistent domestic dominance, regularly winning the Scottish Cup and league together, that often resulted in the third-placed team benefiting from guaranteed European football until Christmas. This elevated the importance of a third-placed finish in a way it hadn't been before.

Aberdeen and Hearts had traded blows over third spot since 2022. Hearts were the first team to benefit from the lucrative rewards of finishing third, in 2021/22, before Aberdeen were the ones making waves on the continent the following year. Struggling to cope with the demands of Europe, the Dons struggled to deal with playing Thursday and Sunday, and it was Hearts who capitalised, once again finishing third in 2023/24. Naturally, this intensified the debate over who can claim to be Scotland's biggest club outside of the Glasgow two. Hearts supporters, despite enduring two relegations since the turn of the 2010s, have seen finishes of third twice since 2020, along with burgeoning attendances, as reasons to believe that they are the third force. Defining what makes one club 'bigger' than another is inherently complex, and achieving consensus among rival supporters on such parameters is impossible. However, if you look at the history of the two clubs since the Second World War, one clearly stands above the other. One of the clubs has 20 major honours, including two European trophies, and the other has ten – no clues for guessing which is which. Regardless, in the face of common sense, this debate persists, further intensifying the significance of matches between the two teams.

Therefore, for both sides, this was as big as it gets – a Hampden showdown with a place in the Scottish Cup Final at stake. Remarkably, it signified the first time Aberdeen and Hearts had met at the national stadium in almost three decades, their last encounter coming in the 1996 semi-final when the Jambos edged a 2-1 win. That such meetings had become so rare felt strange, especially given that both clubs were continuously vying for the mantle of the best of the rest and had reached the semi-final stage together four times since, always kept apart. But this time fate had other plans.

As now seems customary in the build-up to matches at Hampden, ticket allocations and sales seem to dominate the discourse. The Red Army is famous for the excellent away backing they consistently give the team, regularly selling out away ends across the country every week – no small feat given the distances involved. Yet when it comes to Hampden fixtures they are frequently dealt a tough hand. Kick-off times, largely dictated by television broadcasters and local authorities, seldom favour the supporters making the long journey south. Despite these challenges, Aberdeen boast a core Hampden following of around 12,000, an excellent figure that represents roughly 68 per cent of Pittodrie's average home attendance – and that's before factoring in the

300-mile round trip required to get there. Still, opposition fans are often quick to cast judgment on those numbers. For the 12.30pm Saturday kick-off against Hearts on Easter weekend, the Tynecastle club had sold over 20,000 tickets, while Aberdeen were backed by 13,000 travelling fans. Chairman Dave Cormack was quick to defend the support: 'Listen, if today's game was played at Peterhead, it would have been the opposite. We'd have had 25,000 fans.' It wouldn't be the last time he would have to broach the topic of ticket allocations.

Attendances do not win matches, and for that reason it was Aberdeen who were billed as the favourites for the semi-final. The week prior had seen the conclusion of the pre-split fixtures in the Premiership, and Hearts, despite a mid-season rally, couldn't find the all-important victory they needed to squeeze into the top six. A goalless draw with Motherwell, while disgruntled with the overall style of football and impotence in attack, had the Hearts support calling for the head of manager Neil Critchley, who had only been in the post for six months. With a bottom-six finish already confirmed, the Scottish Cup represented Hearts' sole pathway into Europe – and, for Critchley, perhaps the only thread keeping him in the job. Defeat to Aberdeen could well have sealed his fate. On the other side, Thelin characteristically concerned himself with none of this. In the build-up he marked his one-year anniversary since being announced as Aberdeen's new manager, and his first 12 months in charge had been nothing short of a rollercoaster. With only one defeat in eight games, the team was rebuilding its confidence little by little and looked to have kept the wolves, who had been closing in during the winless run, from the door. A dominant display against Rangers the week before the semi-final saw Aberdeen romp to a 2-0 half-time lead but a combination of poor finishing and some strange tactical tweaks from Thelin saw the Glasgow side escape Pittodrie with a point. It was a microcosm of the Dons' season – brilliant one moment and then desperate the next.

Despite the inconsistencies, Thelin now had the opportunity to become the first Dons boss since fellow Scandinavian Ebbe Skovdahl in 2000 to guide Aberdeen to the Scottish Cup Final at the first attempt. Level-headed as ever, he expected his players to learn from their previous semi-final appearance, that horrible mauling by Celtic: 'The best way to learn to manage these kinds of games is to live them and to be there. We have had some big games this season, and I think the more exposure you get to this as a player, the more used to it you get. [As a player] you should just try to do the normal things really well. It's one thing to talk about it after but the next time the pressure comes we have to do better to keep doing the basics well all of the time.'

Although Aberdeen went into the match as favourites, the erratic nature of both teams suggested that it was going to be a tense affair. The inclusion of imposing Bulgarian stopper Dimitar Mitov in the starting 11 for the first time in a month went some way to alleviating some of the pre-match nerves of the Dons support. Ross Doohan had been a capable deputy; however, Mitov carried more of a presence in the box and was the club's undisputed number one. Getting him back for such a vital game was a huge boost.

Despite being outnumbered, the Aberdeen fans, housed in the East Stand, welcomed their team on to the pitch in fine voice, more than matching the 20,000-strong Hearts support. A small pocket of red flares was sparked up, enshrouding Hampden in red smoke as the teams got the match under way. It was Hearts who started on the front foot as they turned the screw on Aberdeen, who struggled to escape the confines of their own half inside the first 20 minutes. However, Thelin's team, sporting their granite grey kit, soaked up the pressure and hit Hearts with a sucker punch. Pape Guèye towered above all around him from a Leighton Clarkson corner to crash a header off the bar. As the ball rebounded, it struck the back of Hearts veteran Craig Gordon in goal and trundled into the net. The roar from the Red Army, delayed as they tried to work out what was happening up the opposite end, echoed around the national stadium. Aberdeen were ahead in a Scottish Cup semi-final for the first time since Adam Rooney had put them 1-0 up after 12 seconds against Hibs in 2017.

Confidence surged through the players. They should have doubled their lead when Morris showcased his blistering pace to round Gordon before clipping the ball to the back post for the onrushing Guèye, but Cammy Devlin popped up to make a crucial intervention and deny the Senegalese his second of the match. Aberdeen looked in total control, something rather unnerving for the fans, who had become accustomed to seeing their side fall apart at the national stadium. However, normal service was resumed after half an hour when Lawrence Shankland was inexplicably left unmarked in the box as the ball was swung in from out wide. The striker controlled with his chest and then lashed under the frame of Mitov to restore parity. Just as it looked as if the game would remain on a knife-edge going into the break, it turned on its head. Guèye, again causing problems for Hearts, picked up a pocket of space in the middle of the park and flicked a neat header into the path of winger Topi Keskinen. The 22-year-old, his explosive pace reminiscent of an Olympic sprinter, ignited the afterburners and sped away from centre-back Michael Steinwender. The Austrian defender, lunging, ended up in a tangle of legs with the Finn, who came crashing to the floor. Referee John Beaton had no option other than to show him a straight red card for the denial of a clear goalscoring opportunity. With a man advantage, Aberdeen were in the driving seat.

If the supporters were expecting their team to come flying out of the traps, smelling blood, then they would be sorely let down. Critchley made moves to shore up his backline at half-time, making two substitutions which saw two forward players make way for two defenders. Under Thelin, Aberdeen had shown that they were a better team when the opposition dominated possession, instead thriving on quick transitions and being able to exploit the space in behind opposing teams with the pace of Keskinen and Morris. Playing against ten men offered the opposite. Their discomfort with the ball showed throughout the second half as they looked bereft of ideas as to how to breach the resolute Hearts defence. Dabbagh, Okkels, Polvara and McGrath had all been introduced to no avail and the 90 minutes ended at 1-1, so Thelin tried to rally his players on the pitch, urging them to show some more bravery on the ball to stretch the tiring Hearts defence.

With only four minutes left of extra time it looked like a penalty shoot-out was on the way. However, before the 120 minutes were up, Aberdeen's numerical advantage would be extended when Devlin stuck his foot in on Dante Polvara and, having already warned the player a few moments earlier, the referee decided it was one foul too many, brandishing a second yellow card. Hearts were down to nine men. Suddenly, Aberdeen's need became urgent as they looked to put this game to bed before risking losing their two-man advantage in a shoot-out. From the resulting free kick, Clarkson hit the ball straight into the wall and it spun away out towards the touchline. Recognising the opportunity their team had with just minutes remaining, a guttural roar, encouraging their side to come again, rumbled out of the east side of Hampden from the Aberdeen fans.

Jack Milne, on as a substitute, prevented the ball from going out and touched it to Jamie McGrath. Hearts, despite their lack of numbers, somehow managed to double up out wide, and McGrath poked the ball back infield. Clarkson found himself standing back over the ball, and as Hearts shuffled their shape, desperately trying to close the gaps, McGrath, who had held his position out wide, was in acres of space. Clarkson spotted him and flicked an outside-of-the-foot pass back into his feet. The Irishman took one touch and whipped a low ball into the box. Milne, who had drifted towards goal, diverted the cross goalwards, but Gordon got down low to parry back into the six-yard box. There, waiting, was Palestinian Oday Dabbagh, who, with the entirety of the gaping goal staring him in the face, stabbed the ball high into the roof of the net from three yards out. Bedlam ensued. Dabbagh, chased by his team-mates, careered over to the red mass bouncing behind the goal, limbs everywhere, his arms outstretched as if embracing the 13,000 Dons fans as one. From being seconds away from a nerve-shredding penalty shoot-out, Aberdeen were now seconds away from a famous victory.

Thelin had spoken pre-match about wanting to see his players deal with 'moments' better, and they did him proud, seeing out the remaining few minutes with ease. Aberdeen were into the Scottish Cup Final for just the third time this century. The Red Army, who had made the early trip to Glasgow, had been rewarded with a last-minute winner and a goal that would be talked about by all who were there for years to come. As 'Country Roads' blared over the tannoy, the players and management headed over to the Dons support to thank them for sticking with the team, not just on the day but over the challenging last few months as well. Everyone connected with Aberdeen celebrated as one, and the camaraderie between the fans and players was evident, something Thelin had worked so hard to create since his appointment. 'Now that we're in the final, we want to win it,' he said. 'You could hear it after the game – supporters, players, staff – we're all so connected and wanted this so much. It means a lot to me. You don't get many chances in your career to reach big finals or fight at the top of the league, so we have to enjoy it and keep fighting.'

Aberdeen: Mitov, Shinnie, Knoester, Dorrington, Jensen, Palaversa, Clarkson, Keskinen, Guèye, Morris, Nisbet
Subs used: *McGrath, Dabbagh, Okkels, Polvara, Milne, Boyd*

Heart of Midlothian: *Gordon, Penrice, McCart, Steinwender, Forrester, Baningime, Grant, Devlin, Shankland, Kabangu, Wilson*
Subs used: *Halkett, Kent, Kingsley, Khartoum, Drameh, Spittal*

With Aberdeen winning the first of the weekend's semi-finals, they would have to wait until the following day to find out who they would be facing in the end-of-season showpiece occasion as Celtic faced off against bottom-of-the-table St Johnstone. The expected result did not take long to materialise as Celtic romped to a 4-0 half-time lead. It would end 5-0 and seal their place in the final for the third year running, this time alongside Aberdeen for a repeat of the 2017 showdown. The jubilation of beating Hearts gave way to the stark realisation that another trip to Hampden to face Celtic awaited. 'You have to believe,' said Thelin in the aftermath of the semi-final. There were few who did.

8

Down but Not Out

IT'S NO secret that Aberdeen supporters have been starved of glory since the turn of the 20th century. Perhaps it is the result of some Faustian bargain made by the club as it rolled into the 80s – a decade of dominance followed by three and a half of humiliation and heartbreak; Alex Ferguson would go on to become Red Devil in chief in Manchester after all. In the nearly 40 years that have passed since Ferguson departed, Aberdeen had made it to the Scottish Cup Final on just four occasions – the same number that he managed in his eight years at the club. More often than not, fans have found themselves on the outside looking in, parked in front of their television screens at home, watching other clubs lift the trophy that they longed to be reacquainted with. The fact that this year would be different brought a surge of excitement and anticipation. As such, like a switch had been flipped, positivity surged around Pittodrie once more in the aftermath of the semi-final triumph. The gleam that had been ever-present in Jimmy Thelin's eyes throughout the start of the campaign, before dwindling somewhat over winter, was back. Through it all, he had remained calm and kept his composure and had been rewarded with a Scottish

Cup Final in his debut season. The board had never wavered over their Swedish talisman during the severe rocky patch of the season. Their patience and loyalty now appeared justified.

However, with only five league games remaining and the Dons being right in the thick of a fight for third place, talk of the Scottish Cup was parked to one side. As Thelin readied his players for the first of the post-split fixtures, against Hibs at Pittodrie, they were fifth, level on points with Dundee United in fourth and, crucially, only three behind the men from Leith, who were occupying third spot. Aberdeen slipping behind Hibs in the table had seemed an unthinkable scenario given the two teams' contrasting starts to the season; the Dons had been 23 points clear at the end of November, the change in fortunes being able to be traced back to the bonkers 3-3 draw at Easter Road between the two sides. Since then, Hibs had lost just once in the league and now headed north on a 17-game unbeaten run. If Aberdeen still harboured any hopes of pipping Hibs to third spot then nothing other than a win would suffice.

The manner in which the game played out reflected its high-stakes nature, which was more akin to that of a chess match. The two managers on the touchline, Thelin and David Gray, moved their pieces, probing and reacting to what the other was doing. Neither side wanted to over-commit and leave themselves open to a sucker punch, which, for Aberdeen, would end any hopes of catching this seemingly unstoppable green juggernaut. It made for a cagey affair. That was until Kevin Nisbet decided to take matters into his own hands. With the clock ticking into the final ten minutes, Graeme Shinnie found himself out wide and clipped a ball into the box. There wasn't a red shirt in sight, which brought groans from the home end, and Rocky Bushiri was able to clear to the edge of the box. However, he failed to get as much height or distance on the ball as he would have liked, and waiting to benefit was Nisbet. Back-pedalling towards the edge of the 18-yard line, Nisbet cushioned the ball dropping out of the heavens on to his chest. As he toppled backwards, he lashed out with his right boot. Time seemed to freeze as the ball arced high over the three Hibs defenders rooted in the box – and, crucially, over the despairing reach of goalkeeper Jordan Smith. All he could do was crane his neck and watch in resignation as the strike dipped perfectly into the top corner.

As one, Pittodrie jumped to its feet in awe. Nisbet himself looked stunned as he wheeled away with his face expressing as much shock as the rest of the stadium as to what he had just done – the striker would later describe the goal as the best of his career. Even the usual dulcet tones of Willie Miller on the radio gave way to screaming disbelief as he bellowed 'KEVIN NISBET! KEVIN! KEVIN NISBET!' down his microphone. The goal would be the only one of the match and drag Aberdeen level on points with Hibs, ending their incredible unbeaten run in the process. It felt like a huge moment in the season, much in the same way as beating Rangers 2-1 had earlier in the campaign. However, the highs of that night at Pittodrie against the Gers would prove short-lived, and Thelin would be hoping to avoid similar on this occasion. If football offers euphoric highs like a drug, then what followed was the inevitable crash – the comedown. The hard-fought victory over Hibs, which had Pittodrie dreaming of third place and guaranteed European group-stage football, quickly gave way to a sense of dismay and unravelling disappointment.

Just as a trip to Paisley halted Aberdeen's invincible run in November, St Mirren would have another notable say in the fortunes of Aberdeen's season. An uninspiring display, comparable to all their recent ones in the town, saw the Dons go down 1-0, despite thinking they had taken the lead, only for VAR to intervene. In Edinburgh, Hibs had bounced back from their Pittodrie disappointment with a resounding 3-1 win over Dundee United, which meant the gap between the two was back to three points, with Hibs holding a far superior goal difference. It meant that Aberdeen realistically needed to take something from their trip to Ibrox to keep their hopes of a third-placed finish alive.

Given the run of form that Rangers found themselves tangled up in heading towards the conclusion of the season, a positive result for Aberdeen looked more likely than would usually be the case. Rangers had not won any of their previous seven home matches, which had included defeats to Hibs, St Mirren, Motherwell and Queen's Park. With Celtic having already wrapped up the league title, Ibrox was littered with empty seats for the clash with Aberdeen. The home crowd had seen enough of their team for the season and wanted nothing more to do with them. It was music to the ears of Aberdeen and Thelin – or so you would have thought. A lacklustre first half ended 0-0, in which neither team managed to threaten. However, an error-strewn Aberdeen collapsed in the second period, Rangers – managed by Dons fans' long-time adversary Barry Ferguson – waltzing to a 4-0 victory. The same players who had been unable to breach the defence of Queen's Park in the Scottish Cup just a few weeks prior had battered Aberdeen, who looked all at sea. It was a confidence-sapping result and a hammer blow to any hopes of third. The way in which their team had crumbled had Aberdeen fans up in arms, and, for the first time, Thelin was coming under some serious fire. These were just some of the fans who had written in to the BBC Sport website:

> 'The same old story of Aberdeen struggling to get a decent result in Glasgow. Add to that a defensive collapse, along with the now almost customary loss of a goal in added time. If all that wasn't enough we have "Softly, softly Jimmy Thelin" churning out the same excuses and promises of it being better in the future.'

> 'I am glad I don't have a final ticket, as I would not want to spend a small fortune to travel to Glasgow and stay there two nights for a guaranteed big loss.'

> 'Simply not good enough, nor any pride wearing the shirt. Simply not fit to wear the once proud shirt of Aberdeen. A cup final hammering awaits. God help us.'

In the bowels of Ibrox, Thelin locked his players in the away dressing room for a lengthy post-mortem in which he lost his cool with the group. When he did appear to do his media rounds, as was his style, he didn't give much away. Captain Graeme Shinnie revealed a few days later that the heated discussions had focused on adhering to the plan and not becoming overly emotional in the face of adversity. Maintaining composure when dealing with setbacks was something Thelin had always emphasised to his players at every club he had been at. 'When things weren't going well, he was a very calm and collected person,' revealed

Fredric Fendrich, who played under Thelin for three years at Jönköping-Södra. 'He was very good at continuing what we wanted to do, the way we wanted to play, and not just abandoning it when things were tough. He trusted his way of playing, and he trusted the players. He was always looking forward and gave us the mantra of always focusing on the next game.' The current problem Thelin had was that the next game was Celtic.

There was no time for Aberdeen to wallow in self-pity as they welcomed the league winners to Pittodrie just three days later, in what was a dress rehearsal for the Scottish Cup Final. It would be the final time the Dons would take to their home turf that season, and they were hopeful of speeding the Red Army on their way to Hampden, via Tannadice, in high spirits. If Thelin was hoping to get the measure of his opponents ahead of the cup final then his hopes would have been dashed when the teams were announced, the visitors making eight changes from the previous week. Anyone looking at the starting XI for Celtic that night knew immediately that it would be an entirely different team that would be starting at Hampden in just a few weeks' time. Even then, Aberdeen struggled against the reserve side Brendan Rodgers had named, and it was the latter who laid down a marker ahead of the final. Celtic, despite the raft of changes, swept home five goals without breaking a sweat, running the hosts ragged in a 5-1 trouncing. The defeat was a humiliating blow for Aberdeen, extinguishing any flicker of hope among their supporters for the upcoming cup final. The team and coaching staff coalesced in the centre circle after the full-time whistle, shellshocked and probably wondering how on earth they were meant to find a chink in this Celtic side's armour.

Elsewhere, Hibs had drawn away in Paisley, putting them four points ahead of Aberdeen, making it mathematically impossible for them to be caught. Fourth place was now the best the Dons could hope for, along with a potential route into the Europa League qualifiers. Even that, though, wasn't guaranteed just yet. Aberdeen still had a job to finish. All they had to do was avoid defeat against Dundee United, who had lost every one of their post-split fixtures, at Tannadice on the final day of the season.

Reflecting on the last ten months as a whole as they headed down the A90, any level-headed supporter would have surmised that a return to European football, a League Cup semi-final, and a Scottish Cup Final still to come was a decent return for Thelin's first season in Scotland. If you had taken Aberdeen's results and shuffled them about, it would have been a more than acceptable campaign. It was the optics of it that painted the second half of the season as a disaster. Given that the Dons had actually won the same number of games as Hibs, who the media had been waxing lyrical about since January, it was far from a catastrophic season. However, the form since winter was still a major cause for concern, and momentum was against the Dons. Even throughout the early season winning streak Thelin had been keen to remind everyone that this was a three-year project, perhaps evidence that he himself had spotted the frailties among this squad early on. The weak mentality that the boss had called out over the winter period had now seeped back into the squad, and it was proving impossible to eradicate.

If you had offered Thelin a straight shoot-out for fourth spot on the final day of the season before a ball had been kicked in anger back in August then he probably would have taken it. Despite the woes of previous weeks, the Red

Army sold out their Tannadice allocation as they looked to roar on the team one final time in the league season – it looked as if it gave the team the boost they needed. Jeppe Okkels, Thelin's star man from his Elfsborg days, slotted home, finally grabbing his first goal of the season after VAR had ruled out his previous two. The opener not only put Aberdeen in the driving seat but also carried extra weight, making Okkels the Dons' 19th different scorer of the season – a new club record. Turning on the style, Thelin's team really should have been a couple of goals further ahead as the half-time whistle blew. The football had been fantastic, begging the question of where this level of performance had been for the last month. Then, just as it had all season, something flipped, and Aberdeen's inconsistent tendencies were apparent for all to see.

Roles were reversed in the second half as Dundee United upped the intensity and Aberdeen struggled to stifle the momentum of the hosts. The Dons' defensive deficiencies were then laid bare as former player Declan Gallagher popped a simple header from a corner into the net for the hosts – it was far too easy. Six minutes later, the pendulum had completely swung: Dundee United were awarded a penalty, and striker Sam Dalby sent Mitov the wrong way to leapfrog Aberdeen in the live table into fourth place. It was another dispiriting collapse and, despite a late flurry of chances, Aberdeen never looked like salvaging the draw they needed to finish fourth – the league season ended with a whimper.

It had started in unbelievable fashion with 15 straight wins and talk of a title race before completely falling apart. Since mid-November Aberdeen had been the worst team in the league, winning just five of their last 27 league matches and picking up a miserable 22 points from a possible 87. Finishing with a -13 goal difference, which highlighted its own problems, ensured that Aberdeen slipped behind Dundee United to end the season in fifth. Hundreds of home fans, their emotions getting the better of them, spilled on to the pitch at the end of the game, some of them making their way towards and goading the visiting supporters housed in the top of the Jerry Kerr Stand. The ugly scenes saw the players on the pitch crowded by opposition fans before they had a chance to escape down the tunnel – a situation that rarely ends well. As the taunting intensified, some projectiles started to rain down on the Dundee United fans. In a horrible incident, Aberdeen substitute Jack MacKenzie was struck in the head with a chair that someone had ripped out and thrown. MacKenzie, visibly hurt and distraught by the situation, was whisked down the tunnel on a stretcher by medical staff, needing stitches both above and below his eye, such was the seriousness of the injury. 'Everything is quite dark right now,' said Thelin after the game, also expressing his anger at the treatment MacKenzie had received. 'But it's also my job to look to the future in an optimistic way.'

In the aftermath, Aberdeen released a club statement condemning the actions that had unfolded. A season that began with dazzling promise ended in disarray as the mood veered from triumph to turmoil – it was the worst possible preparation for a cup final. Thelin had an almighty task to pick up the spirits of his players for a date with Celtic at Hampden in six days' time. How was he supposed to reverse the fortunes of his struggling side in under a week? Aberdeen had hit the canvas hard – Dundee United had landed another telling blow. As they staggered back to their feet, for all the world it looked as if Celtic were poised to deliver the final knockout inside the ropes of Hampden. But they refused to stay down. Nobody – not even Aberdeen supporters – gave them a fighting chance. Crucially, though, the fight wasn't over yet.

9

Hope Over Expectation

THERE HAVE been shocks abound in the 139 years that the Scottish Cup has been contested. Inverness Caledonian Thistle famously went ballistic at Celtic Park at the turn of the millennium; Highland League Brora Rangers humiliated Hearts in 2021; Aberdeen were downed by lowly Darvel; and Rangers, most recently of all, were humbled by Queen's Park on their own patch. However, when it comes to the final itself, it is so often the expectant victor who walks up the famed Hampden steps to lift the trophy. On this occasion, even more so than any who had come before, underdogs Aberdeen had been completely written off. For the supporters, desperate to push against the tide of green-and-white puissance, making the case for their team to produce an upset was an impossible task.

Celtic's record against Aberdeen throughout the course of the season had been almost impeccable, the only blot on the jotter that 2-2 draw at Parkhead in October. In the four encounters since, Brendan Rodgers's men, as if taking affront to the audacity Aberdeen had in turning up to Celtic Park to steal a point, had fired in 17 goals to the Dons' two. A semi-final hammering before a couple of 5-1 victories in both

Glasgow and Aberdeen had followed. It had been a series of morale-sapping hammerings for both the players and the fans. 'The perception was in the media that Aberdeen had zero chance and zero possibility of winning the 2025 Scottish Cup,' observed journalist Graham Spiers. 'For Aberdeen, one of the great Scottish clubs, to be so heavily unfancied was an astonishing scenario. There have only been a handful of finals where one team had been so heavily fancied over the other. I covered the 1995 final, where nobody gave Airdrie a prayer against Celtic, and the other one that springs to mind is Queen of the South against Rangers in 2008 – both of those clubs had been in the Second Division at the time. This game was well up there with the preconceived one-sided final in which Aberdeen hardly stood a chance.' The last Scottish Cup Final in which you could feasibly point to the underdog overcoming the odds was Dundee United in 1994, beating a treble-seeking Rangers under Walter Smith – that was 31 years earlier.

After the teams had secured their place in the final with their respective April semi-final victories, Celtic were instantly installed as the overwhelming favourites to clinch the prize for the third consecutive year. In the ensuing weeks, their prospects shifted from that of strong contenders to some suggesting that they may as well already have their name engraved on the trophy, as Aberdeen lurched from one disaster to the next, culminating in the horrendous scenes at Tannadice. 'The previous weekend had been awful, with the Dundee United game and the [Jack] Mackenzie incident,' said Aberdeen-supporting reporter Michael Grant. 'There was so much negativity around everything to do with Aberdeen after that, and then you're looking at the cup final thinking, "What is this going to be!?" At that point, it was hard to see a turnaround in fortunes in a week. There were people predicting three, four or five-nil. I remember listening to a couple of Aberdeen fans' podcasts and they were all pretty downbeat, clutching at straws over how we could somehow win the final.'

Supporter Matt Findlay summed up the feeling among the fanbase: 'I, along with every other Dons fan, was apprehensive in the sense that we could get absolutely battered in the same way that we did in the semi-final. That game could quite easily have scarred the players in the back of their minds, which it looked like it had, going by the other games against Celtic that season. My dad, who goes to every home game and has been to all of the cup finals over the years, said to me, "I don't know if I can do it, I don't know if I can go [to the final], as I don't want to feel that horrible disappointment again."'

There was something much more deep-rooted to those fears and anxieties than the recent poor run of results. When it came to facing Celtic at Hampden, or anywhere really, Aberdeen were battle-fatigued – every occasion producing a new, indelible scar, its effects burning deep into the Dons' psyche. Aberdeen hadn't beaten Celtic at Hampden since 1992 – a League Cup semi-final – and in the ten clashes there since, they had been overly innovative in finding new ways to lose every single time. The first of those nine came in the 2000 League Cup Final, the first final of the new millennium to be played at Hampden. The Red Army brought the noise and the colour and, even if the effort was matched by the players on the pitch, it wouldn't be enough. Aberdeen, lacking quality and cutting edge, failed to trouble Celtic, who ran out comfortable 2-0 winners, Ebbe Skovdahl's side playing the last half an hour with ten men after Thomas Solberg was ordered off. 'If ever there was a day when Dons fans deserved better this was it,' wrote former sports editor Charlie Allan in the *Aberdeen Evening Express*. 'I have been to Hampden on many occasions, a fair few of them as a member of the Red Army, but I have never heard the Aberdeen fans in better voice.' It would become a familiar story.

In 2011, after Craig Brown had taken over from the disastrous spell of Mark McGhee, Aberdeen would undergo two chastening Hampden outings against Celtic. The first was a League Cup semi-final where they found themselves 4-0 down after 35 minutes, all but ending the game as a contest. The Scottish Cup semi-final saw Andrew Considine red-carded after only 18 minutes, and again the fans faced another long, depressing journey back up the road after shipping four goals without reply. The 2016/17 season saw red and green clash again at Hampden. Despite gathering at the halfway line to face down Celtic's huddle in defiance, Aberdeen were swept aside 3-0 with ease in the one-sided League Cup Final. The Dons returned later that season for the Scottish Cup Final – their first in 17 years. It ended in heartbreak, Tom Rogic putting Aberdeen to the sword with just seconds remaining. Two seasons later, Aberdeen would lose out yet again to Celtic. In a cruel twist of fate, Ryan Christie, who had spent 18 months on loan in the north-east, would come back to haunt the Dons, scoring the only goal of the game to see Rodgers's team claim their seventh domestic trophy in a row. Four months later, Aberdeen would lose 3-0 in the Scottish Cup semi-final to the same opponents, this time ending with nine men. By that point losing to Celtic at Hampden felt like a yearly custom, coming around as sure as Christmas does every year – the perverse enjoyment coming solely from predicting how the Dons would manage to lose on each occasion.

COVID-19 brought the entire world to a standstill in 2020, but even that couldn't halt Aberdeen's Hampden hoodoo against the Hoops. The delayed Scottish Cup resumed in November and Aberdeen once again lost to Celtic at the semi-final stage, behind closed doors as a result of the ongoing restrictions – at least the Red Army didn't have to make the obligatory wasted journey for this one. The 2024 semi-final, featuring a bruised Aberdeen, under the temporary leadership of Peter Leven, saw them drag Celtic all the way to penalties in a thrilling match. They had shown unbelievable character, scoring at the end of 90 minutes and then again after 120 to force a penalty shoot-out – it had sparked unbelievable scenes among the pocket of 12,000 Aberdeen fans who had braved the occasion. However, it again ended in disappointment with Celtic prevailing after a questionable display of shot-stopping from goalkeeper Kelle Roos. The most recent encounter, the 6-0 hammering back in November had ended Aberdeen's unbeaten start to the season and shattered their confidence. Taking all of that into account, coupled with the way in which Aberdeen had ended the league campaign, you could have forgiven the supporters for being more than a little uneasy at the thought of another showdown with Celtic in the south side of Glasgow.

'As a fan you can look at the records, recent form and think that realistically there's not really a chance of getting anything here – as a player you just cannot do that,' said Brian Irvine, the hero the last time Aberdeen defeated Celtic in a cup final. 'You still have to have the belief in yourself that you can go and win. When you are out on the pitch, you can affect the game and the outcome, so you have to be positive. If you are going into any game thinking you are going to lose, then there's no point in turning up.'

If there was one thing Jimmy Thelin would have been doing in the build-up to the cup final, it was drilling that belief into his players, trying to convince them that this time, with this game plan, they could hurt Celtic. It was never going to be an easy sell, but his responsibility was to lift the dressing room ahead of what would be the biggest game of many of the players' careers – an opportunity Thelin was determined they would not let slip. Ten years earlier, when he was the head coach at Jönköping-Södra in the Swedish second tier, the team had fired out of the blocks, losing just one of their opening 14 matches. It put the perennial mid-tablers in with a shot at the title. As the season entered the closing months, J-Södra stumbled, dropping points in five of their last eight games, allowing Graham Potter's Östersund back into the fight. However, as he prepared his team for the final match of the season, Thelin knew a win would be enough to seal the title. 'Thelin wanted to build a long-term culture where you created winners,' explained Frederic Fendrich, a key player for J-Södra during that title showdown. 'With the help of principles, strong camaraderie and ideas, he created an atmosphere in the team where we took care of each other first and foremost as humans and then also as players. All the players adapted to this quite quickly and the results also came with it. During the season the bubble that we stayed in helped create this togetherness.' The unity that Thelin had instilled shone through in the end, with J-Södra winning their final game 5-2 to clinch first place and, with it, their return to the Allsvenskan for the first time in 46 years.

Preparing for his first cup final as a manager, Thelin needed to leverage all his experience if he was to achieve what would be a monumental upset. Crucially, he also had to instil the belief in his players that lifting the trophy could be a reality – it was within touching distance. Throughout the week, in training sessions, meetings and discussions, Thelin consistently declared 'when we win the final' to his players, avoiding any hint of the doubts that may have been rattling around his mind. As all good leaders should, he was subtly yet effectively building confidence within the squad, a belief that solidified as the week progressed. By the time he spoke to the media, he and his players had forgotten all that had gone before and were fixated on coming out on the right side of history. 'I think you have to move on [from the last Celtic game],' Thelin told reporters. 'This is a final. Of course we learn things from the game, but this is a final, this is a different kind of game. When you feel the spirit amongst the players, they are looking forward to the game, you can feel the belief amongst them. So the other game is in the past, this is the final, and it's the only thing we can feel in front of us. I think in the football world you always have to have strong belief, and dream big. Let's see.'

The media balked at the notion of Thelin believing anything other than a Celtic walkover. In the week leading up to the cup final, plenty of articles and opinion pieces were published, all of them predicting a comfortable Celtic victory, which would see them claim their sixth domestic treble in nine seasons. In the eyes of the media Aberdeen's form had them nothing more than the supporting cast in what would be Celtic's day of glory. While the newspapers and journalists had a job to do in putting forward the narrative around the final of everything pointing towards a Celtic victory, some of the reporting and comments crossed a line that showed a lack of respect for Thelin and the Dons. Below are just some of the opprobrious lines that were published in the week leading up to the game:

Kris Boyd in *The Sun*: 'Just wait, Aberdeen's players will soon be telling anyone who'll listen that they're ready to put up a fight against Celtic in the Scottish Cup Final. No they won't. At Hampden next Saturday afternoon, Jimmy Thelin's Dons will be lambs to the slaughter. They'll vow to show some backbone. But I'm sorry, for as long as anyone can remember they've been spineless when it's come to this fixture.'

Keith Jackson in the *Daily Record*: 'This one could get very messy for an Aberdeen side which had six goals taken off it the last time they met Celtic at Hampden in the League Cup semis. Something similar awaits now that the champions have another domestic treble within touching distance. Aberdeen 0 Celtic 5.'

Daily Record: 'Aberdeen vs Celtic may be the biggest ever Scottish Cup Final hammering as fears grow old record could be smashed.'

John McGarry in the *Daily Mail*: 'Because Thelin is so tactically inflexible, opposition teams can read Aberdeen like a book. There are no surprises, nothing sprung from left field for other coaches to consider.'

It had indeed been 30 games since Aberdeen last beat Celtic – a 1-0 win at Celtic Park in 2018. However, even if it did seem inconceivable that it would be Graeme Shinnie lifting the trophy instead of Callum McGregor, the disrespectful tone was noted by the Red Army and the cry in response was to stick it on the proverbial dressing room wall. The entirety of Scottish football anticipated a Celtic treble and, relegating the Dons to nothing more than a footnote in a cup final that had yet to be played, galvanised the aggrieved Aberdeen supporters, who were ready to set aside all that had gone before in a bid to get behind their team for one last time that season.

The club itself wasn't ready to go down without a fight either, and the first battle of the Scottish Cup Final would be fought within the offices across Hampden and Pittodrie. Once the two finalists had been set following the semi-finals, the Scottish Football Association contacted Aberdeen to inform them of the ticket allocation that they would receive. It was to be 16,500 tickets, which would see their fans – as usual when facing off against Celtic – housed in the West Stand, with the Glasgow support given the entirety of the North Stand. For those not in tune with Scottish football, two clubs have unofficially designated ends at the national stadium. If Aberdeen are playing Celtic, they'll be in the West Stand – if it's Rangers, they'll be in the East. The same goes for every other club in Scotland, and, as such, the East and West wings of Hampden Park are more commonly known as the 'Celtic end' and 'Rangers end'. For what is a supposed neutral venue it's a situation that angers fans of the clubs outside of Glasgow's big two. Could you imagine Wembley had a 'Manchester United end' and a 'Liverpool end'? It simply wouldn't happen.

Chairman Dave Cormack, no stranger to rocking the apple cart in Scottish football, had tested Hampden chiefs a few years prior on the archaic tradition, asking for a toss of the coin over which ends Rangers and Aberdeen fans should be allocated for the 2023 League Cup Final. Unsurprisingly, his request was turned down. Aberdeen had also been denied a fair split of the tickets on that occasion. However, defiant and refusing to accept his club's place as a sideshow for Scotland's showpiece occasion, Cormack was not willing to bow to what he saw as unfair treatment of the Dons' loyal supporters. Cormack hit back at the SFA's offer, demanding that Aberdeen be handed half of the tickets – something a vast swathe of fans across Scotland argue should be standard for every game at a neutral venue. An exact split of tickets was not something that the SFA were prepared to do, instead offering Aberdeen just over 20,000, which would see fans populate half of the North Stand up to the halfway line – but with a caveat. The offer was contingent on Aberdeen having to underwrite the cost of any unsold tickets. Confident of the Red Army's strong backing, it was an offer Cormack acquiesced to.

Accepting the proposal was only viable due to the robust financial standing Cormack had established for Aberdeen since becoming chairman in 2019. Other clubs in a less secure financial position would have been compelled to accept fewer tickets, highlighting the absurd nature of the SFA's handling of the ticket distribution. When the situation became public, it was a PR victory for the club and Cormack. He had fought tooth and nail to get his supporters as many tickets as possible and they responded with gusto, selling out the entire allocation in a single day. As usual, the Red Army had delivered when the club had needed them most and would now occupy almost half of Hampden – Cormack had been vindicated. It was the catalyst for a groundswell of resistance from the supporters. With the 20,000 tickets secured, fan group Ultras Aberdeen launched their 'All in Red at Hampden' campaign, calling on all fellow supporters with a ticket for the match to wear something red to create an imposing wall of colour on the day. Concurrently, they were busy fundraising and planning for one of the most audacious tifos ever executed by the Red Army. The ultras targeted raising £10,000 for the planned display and were sped well on their way to the target after Cormack himself generously donated £1,000 to the cause. By the time the cup final rolled around, the fundraiser had smashed its goal, with over 500 donations in total, Dons fans once again showing why they are some of the best in the country.

With the ticket fiasco negotiated, thoughts began to turn to the game itself. Aberdeen's chances had been laid bare. The bookmakers made them 9/1 outsiders, the media gave them no hope and supporters of other clubs were already rolling their eyes at Celtic securing yet another domestic trophy. The psyche of a football fan inhabits two ends of a spectrum – either overly optimistic or excessively gloom-ridden. Throughout the build-up to the final, Aberdeen supporters flicked between the two. The Monday following the Dundee United disaster had them in agreement that it would be a Hampden massacre – by Thursday, they were wondering, what if? Mankind has looked to the skies for signs of hope and answers since time began. Ahead of the cup final, Dons supporters did the same.

Across the world of sport, 2025 was proving to be the year of the underdog. Newcastle United claimed their first trophy in 56 years, while Crystal Palace got their hands on their first piece of silverware in the way of the FA Cup. Tottenham Hotspur won the Europa League to end their 17-year trophy drought; on the continent, Lewis Ferguson's Bologna ended their 51-year wait for the Coppa Italia, Go Ahead Eagles in the Netherlands got their first major honour in 93 years, while VfB Stuttgart won the German Cup, their first major title in 18 years. Would fate see to add Aberdeen's name to the list? It was certainly something, anything to grasp on to.

In submitting his match preview for the morning of the cup final for *The Times*, Michael Grant, even though being relatively despondent about Aberdeen's chances, found that positive undertones were threatening to break through. 'I was looking back on the preview that I wrote for the Saturday morning; it was quite downbeat on Aberdeen's chances. However, the online headline was "How underdogs Aberdeen can spoil Celtic's treble party", and I'd love to say that that was the overall tone of the piece, but it wasn't really. But if you see the headline, that makes it look like I had an inkling that we would do something. Well, the only thing I could claim – in terms of my preview, which did kind of predict a Celtic win – was that I did think Aberdeen could hurt Celtic because we'd scored four times against them in the previous games, albeit we'd lost a heap of goals at the same time. So, I took some hope from the fact that they had been able to score against Celtic, but because of the recent form and the recent results, I couldn't see it. And also, of course, Thelin had just played that one system, that one style all season – he'd tried to be open and tried to go for it, and I just don't suppose any of us were really sure whether he would change that.'

In truth, it felt like an act of divine intervention, rather than that of a formation change, would be needed for Aberdeen to stand any chance of prevailing. As part of the coverage in the days leading up to the final, BBC Scotland had Willie Miller sit down with Jimmy Thelin in the Pittodrie boardroom for a one-on-one interview. 'How do you beat Celtic?' posed the club legend. 'I hope you can see that on Saturday,' laughed Thelin. The unflappable Swede seemed to have emerged from the self-confessed darkness that he had found himself in just a week before and appeared surprisingly optimistic: 'The good thing is that we have a clear idea of what we want to do now ... we have a clear strategy and we just have to execute it on Saturday.' There was a sparkle in Thelin's eyes as he spoke, exuding a confidence that belied Aberdeen's appalling end to the season. On the eve of the big game, the feelings of despair had dissipated somewhat, and a seed of optimism had been planted in what appeared to be the most infertile of grounds. In football, there's always a chance.

So, on 24 May 2025, whether out of blind faith, a flicker of hope, or the sheer sense of duty, over 20,000 Aberdeen fans – decked out all in red – descended on Glasgow once more, carried by hope rather than expectation.

10

Time for New Heroes

*The experience of defeat, or more particularly
the manner in which a leader reacts to it, is
an essential part of what makes a winner.*

Sir Alex Ferguson

Glasgow, 10am

On the morning of 24 May 2025, thousands of Dons fans
were on the march. While the majority headed south from
the Granite City, there were those travelling from places
like Kirkwall, London, the Isle of Man, Canada, and even
as far afield as Australia – all roads led to Hampden. The
20,000-strong contingent would be the largest concentration
of Aberdeen supporters in one place since the 2017 Scottish
Cup Final. Hoping for a better outcome on this occasion,
and despite all that had come before, the Red Army had been
mobilised en masse.

An interminable 35 years had now passed since Brian
Irvine's Scottish Cup Final-winning penalty in 1990. Now,
on the same day he celebrated his 60th birthday, Irvine was
headed for Hampden once more. 'I got myself booked on to
one of the supporters' buses. The feeling among everyone

was that they just hoped the players would make the club proud and put in a good performance; that was all we were asking. Realistically, everyone knew we were just hoping for a moment to celebrate; you'd have been chucked off the bus if you'd suggested we would win it! We were delighted just to be in the final. I don't think any of us genuinely believed we were going to lift the cup.'

However, a glimmer of 'what if?' began to emerge for some fans who dared to dream. This was a one-off game – anything could happen, couldn't it? 'After getting the tickets, my brother couldn't make it in the end, and I was unsure whether to travel on my own to Hampden, to once again watch us get battered by a Brendan Rodgers Celtic team,' said Stewart Smith, an Isle of Man-based Dons fan. 'As the week went on, I couldn't take the thought of us winning and not being there, to the extent I was almost hoping we'd lose if I weren't at Hampden. That's when I knew I had to go. On Friday night at 6pm my partner came home from work. I was holding our 18-month-old as I told her that I had to go and I'd be home Sunday. She was surprisingly supportive! A boat, taxi and train later, I arrived in Glasgow on cup final day at 10am.'

Red shirt after red shirt spilled into Glasgow from all directions, thousands of Aberdeen fans streaming into the city as the hours ticked towards kick-off. Every corner you turned in Glasgow's city centre seemed to reveal another cluster of Dons fans. There were so many of them that it felt as if it would be fitting for the iconic Duke of Wellington statue to forgo the famous traffic cone atop its head for a red bucket hat.

As the Aberdeen fans turned Glasgow red, the men they were pinning their hopes and dreams on were holding their final pre-match meeting. Club captain and Aberdeen-born Graeme Shinnie led the council of war at the team's hotel, reminding his team-mates of just what lifting the trophy would mean to the supporters and city. Back in 2014, he had been on the opposing side when Aberdeen overcame Inverness Caledonian Thistle on penalties to lift the club's first trophy in 19 years. The whole of Aberdeen had flocked to Union Street to welcome home their heroes on that occasion. Shinnie wanted his own piece of history in red and he was determined to drag his team-mates to glory. Jimmy Thelin had revealed earlier in the week how he had been in contact with a familiar face in the north-east of Scotland: 'Sir Alex has been in touch and I have had some advice. He's a really nice gentleman and it's good to talk to him sometimes. It would be nice to follow in his footsteps.' As part of the meeting, a collection of video messages from people across the city was played to the team. One of those featured was the great Sir Alex Ferguson himself. After the most incredible night of his managerial career, in which Manchester United scored two goals in two minutes to win the 1999 Champions League, Ferguson famously said, 'But they never give in, and that's what won it.' His message to the Aberdeen players was similar – in football, there's always a chance, you can never give in. With the personal words of the greatest football manager ever ringing in their ears, the squad set off for Hampden. They were ready to write their own story.

Southside, Glasgow, 1.45pm

As Celtic lashed in goal upon goal at Pittodrie in the final league meeting between the sides that season, it became apparent to Thelin that if Aberdeen were to succeed in the cup final it was imperative that he adopt a different approach. When the teams were announced by Aberdeen's social media accounts, it revealed that Thelin had rolled the dice: the Swede had shifted from his favoured 4-2-3-1 formation and deployed a 5-3-2. It was a move aimed at ensuring defensive stability. The biggest surprise was the inclusion of Jack Milne as the additional centre-half. The Aberdeen-born 22-year-old had only made two starts all season and was now being asked to hold back the green-and-white tide in what was the biggest game of his career. It was a bold move by the manager. Milne was flanked by Alfie Dorrington on his right and Dutchman Mats Knoester on his left, with Alexander Jensen and Nicky Devlin operating as the wing-backs. Critically, that allowed Graeme Shinnie to shift into midfield, away from the full-back position in which he had been run ragged by James Forrest earlier in the month. The skipper had played in all but two of Aberdeen's matches that season, ensuring that when he led his team out on to the Hampden pitch, he would do so making his 300th appearance for the club.

Aberdeen starting XI: Mitov, Jensen, Dorrington, Milne, Knoester, Devlin, Shinnie, Palaversa, Clarkson, Keskinen, Nisbet

As the team news was digested by the anxious fans, a sense of relief washed over them in the first instance – Thelin had mixed it up. 'I remember sitting in the snooker club in Mount Florida before the match with my mates and we were speaking about the game and how we thought it would go,' said supporter Matt Findlay. 'But then the team lines came out, and there was just this silence as everyone took it in. It

felt like a big moment. Everyone was like, "Oh he's done something different," and it was the first time he had really done that all season. I don't know why, but because it was something left field, it felt like a little bit of hope to cling on to. We then came out of the bar, the rain was starting, but through it you could just see a sea of red. Walking to the stadium, we just forget about the rubbish results from the past few weeks. You're surrounded by thousands of other Aberdeen fans and think this is the Scottish Cup Final.'
There was an undoubted buzz of anticipation in the air as a surging tide of red washed towards Hampden as the rain started to fall. Spontaneous choruses of 'Stand Free' and 'Aberdeen Olé Olé Olé' shot up, occasionally swelling into a loud, stirring crescendo. The sheer energy exuded by the Aberdeen faithful made it impossible to discern the trials and tribulations that they had endured up to this point. Expectant, maybe not, but many of them were beseeching the football gods to grant them one day of glory. As if in answer, the heavens opened around 2.30pm over Hampden. A lot has been made about how lightning bolted down from the sky just as Tom Rogic scored his famous goal to dash Aberdeen's dreams in the 2017 Scottish Cup Final. Eight years on, thundery showers had once again been forecast for the occasion. Lightning, surely, couldn't strike twice?

Aberdeen, 2pm

Not everyone, of course, could make it down to Glasgow to cheer on the Dons. Norman Mackay was one of those: 'My son was headed down the road for the game, but I missed out on a ticket. Instead, I was on the way down to Stonehaven on the morning of the game. On the way back to where I stay, I made the point of driving past the spot where my dad's ashes are scattered – he was a huge Dons fan. I promised him that we were going to do it for him, that the Dons were going to lift the cup.' Some stayed at home to watch, some headed down to the packed pubs across the city – the Foundry Bar, which sits at the top of Holburn Street and is one of the best-known Aberdeen supporters' bars, was decorated with even more Dons colours than usual. You could even grab an 'Angus on the Beach' cocktail or a 'Donny the Sheep bomb' to settle the nerves. Almost any pub showing the game had been fully booked out. The Granite City was ready.

Hampden Park, 2.50pm

Hampden has its critics, but little rivals the sweeping bowl-shaped terraces on Scottish Cup Final day. The single-tiered stands make for an impressive sight, bursting with colour and excitement. What became clear early on in this final was that the Aberdeen support appeared to have left any doubts or fears over their team's inhibitions at the turnstiles. The west end of Hampden was packed with thousands of raucous Aberdonians ready to make themselves heard. Before the occasion got under way, the customary parading of the trophy by the respective club icons took place. Representing Aberdeen was Alex McLeish, the last Dons captain to walk up the Hampden steps to lift the trophy. During the week, McLeish had been more optimistic about his old team's chances than most. 'Celtic will be firm favourites but in a one-off game anything can happen,' he told the *Daily Record*. 'I know that from experience when we lifted the cup [the League Cup in 2011] at Birmingham City. Not many people fancied us to beat Arsenal but we did. We went into that game with a strategy and a plan to stifle their attacking players. We worked on it, stuck to it, got a bit of luck and in the end we lifted the cup.' As McLeish hoisted the trophy into the air, a huge cheer went up from the supporters. McLeish, now 66, was an Aberdeen legend from a time gone by. The fans were hoping, and praying, that they would have some new heroes before the day was out.

Inside the Hampden tunnel, the men hoping to become those heroes were assembling. Standing alongside them was ten-year-old Callum, who had been selected as a mascot for the game. His inclusion stemmed from a story first shared on *Sportsound* by his uncle Stuart. Callum's dad, Gordon, a devoted Aberdeen supporter, had sadly passed away shortly after renewing his season ticket for the following campaign. The tale caught the attention of chairman Dave Cormack, who was so moved that he personally reached out to the family. Cormack arranged for Callum to walk out with the players on what promised to be the most unforgettable of occasions. At the head, preparing to lead them out was Jimmy Thelin. Wearing a black formal suit, with a red tie and boutonnière, he looked the part for his first cup final – his cool, composed facial expressions belying the gravitas of the occasion. From the tunnel, you could hear the extraordinary atmosphere bubbling away, and the nerves must have been thrumming through the team. There was no turning back or shirking out now. The referee got the signal, and both sets of players strode out into a pulsating colosseum of noise and red and green.

Hampden Park, 2.55pm

Led by Thelin, Aberdeen were roared on to the pitch by a rambunctious Red Army, who unveiled a stunning tifo of the city's coat of arms. For Dons fans, travelling to Glasgow to play one of the Old Firm isn't just about football; it's about representing a city so often dismissed by the rest of the country. The energy of the entire north-east was compressed into the 'Beach End' of Hampden, willing and waiting. 'Walking out at Hampden as an Aberdeen player is incredible,' said former captain Joe Lewis. 'When the heat from those flames hits your face, it gives you a real buzz. It is a special stadium and always an amazing occasion as you are at the national stadium. When you see all of the Aberdeen fans that have come to back you, it gives you goosebumps as you are walking out for these cup finals.' Stephen McCormick, support experience manager at the club, is one reason why these tifos are such a success. 'The idea for the city crest to be displayed at Hampden for the cup final came from Ultras Aberdeen,' said McCormick. 'Some members of Ultras Aberdeen and I travelled down to Glasgow on Wednesday afternoon so we could make an early start with the design on Thursday morning. It was important that we had the outlines of the design finished in time for the arrival of the volunteers on Friday morning. The club organised a free bus for the volunteers to take them up and down the road to ensure the tifo could be completed. On the day, the participation from the Red Army was fantastic. Of all the years of going to Hampden, that was hands down the best Aberdeen support I have ever been a part of, unbelievable backing all day from the stands.' As the tifo melted away, it revealed behind it a formidable red wall that looked 100ft tall. The 'All in Red' campaign had been heard loud and clear by the Aberdeen fans – it was a spectacular sight. If Celtic thought they would be turning up to roll over a tired and battle-weary Aberdeen, they discovered the opposite. The Dons players would have found it impossible not to be buoyed by the passion and noise generated by their supporters – determined to spur their team on to a famous victory, as unlikely as that may have seemed.

Hampden Park, 3pm

Kick-off. It was the men in red, like the entirety of their support behind them, who got the game under way as the referee's whistle sounded. Graeme Shinnie passed the ball all the way back to Jack Milne, who took one touch and launched it up the field. The direct approach caused some disorder in the Celtic ranks before Cameron Carter-Vickers attempted to pick out Daizen Maeda, so often the hammer of Aberdeen. The Japanese uncharacteristically miscontrolled the ball, which bounced past him and out for a throw-in. The completely insignificant act was met with a massive cheer by the Aberdeen fans. They were fuelled by adrenaline and were going to use every Celtic mishap or misplaced pass to their advantage. Kick-off had been what a lot of the supporters had been dreading all week, but now that it was here, there was a strange expectancy in the air. Deep down, nobody truly believed Aberdeen could come to Hampden and overcome Celtic – not here, not on this stage, not on this day. And yet, from the first whistle, there was a crackle in the air, a sense of destiny hanging heavy over the ground, as if this day was fated to be different.

Hampden Park, 3.25pm

After the frenzied opening few minutes, the game settled into a pattern that many had predicted. Aberdeen had retreated into their own half, Celtic had the ball and were pinging it about, probing for a way through. For Thelin, it was about breaking the match down into stages. Survive the first ten minutes, then get to 20, 30, and so on – every staging post was a step closer to full time. What became apparent in the opening 25 minutes, however, was that Celtic, who had won the league by a vast chasm of 17 points, were not as quick or incisive in possession as they so often had been.

The supporters, getting right behind their team and stopping only to bite at their fingernails, were looking for anything to latch on to for encouragement. When Alfie Dorrington decided to slalom up the left wing with the ball, skipping past three challenges, it brought the fans to life, celebrating the Spurs loanee riding tackles with the same passion as if he had smashed the ball into the back of the net each time. Although the charge came to nothing, it got the players up the pitch and gave the defence some rare respite.

Hampden Park, 3.40pm

Although they were dominating possession, Celtic were struggling. Aberdeen were sitting in their low block and were doing an excellent job of denying their opponents the space. As the clock ticked towards 40 minutes, Celtic's Arne Engels tried to slip in Maeda down the left wing, but Nicky Devlin was all over it and hooked the ball out for a corner. It was Engels himself who whipped in the corner from the left. The looping cross was met by Carter-Vickers, the American leaping highest to beat Jack Milne in the air. The header initially looked to be drifting wide for a goal kick but Dorrington found himself in the wrong place at the wrong time. The ball struck his shoulder, diverting it towards goal and into the back of the net beyond the outstretched Dimitar Mitov.

Aberdeen hands immediately went to heads. It was a strange, unorthodox goal to lose, but that mattered little – Celtic were ahead. Such were the celebrations among the Hoops' players and supporters it was barely noticeable that they had just taken the lead in the Scottish Cup Final. 'Both of my sons were in the Aberdeen end and they thought that the goal had been disallowed,' said journalist Michael Grant. 'The reaction from the Celtic end was so muted that he genuinely thought that it must have been chopped off. That was a common theme on the day; the Celtic supporters seemed pretty subdued. I've been to a million games at Hampden, so I wouldn't say this lightly, but you could tell that the Aberdeen support was far more up for it than the Celtic support. I'm not criticising Celtic for that as I think it's only natural as the occasion was much bigger for us than it was for them.' Despite that, Celtic were once again leading the Dons at Hampden. Worried Aberdonian minds flicked back to the 6-0 game at the end of 2024 – the opening goal to break the deadlock on that occasion had seen Carter-Vickers bullet home a header from an Engels corner. Nicky Devlin could be seen calling for calm among his team-mates, while Thelin, watching on from the sidelines, had spoken all season long about being mentally resilient in challenging moments. A quickfire second never materialised, and the Dons eked over the line at half-time, just a single goal down and still in with a fighting chance.

The West Stand, Hampden Park, 3.55pm

Despite trailing at the break, Aberdeen had limited Celtic to little and had defended resolutely. As Thelin and his staff were giving their team talk, it would be the turn of the fans at the half-time interval to defend the colours. For some reason police and stewards standing in front of the Ultras Aberdeen section decided to snatch away one of the red pole flags that had been proudly flying throughout the game. This didn't go down too well with the wider Aberdeen support. Paper from the pre-match tifo, as well as a chorus of boos, rained down on the gathering crowd of stewards and police behind the goal. Eventually seeing sense, and seemingly to avoid any further issues, the flag was handed back to the fans, which was met by an enormous cheer from those in red and white. It intensified the heat in the already tense atmosphere. As the players, none the wiser as to what had been happening, re-emerged for the second period, they were welcomed back on to the pitch by their supporters with rejuvenated fervour – they were ready to start a fightback in this final.

Hampden Park, 4.05pm

Although Celtic had done little to trouble the Dons, the opening 45 minutes saw Aberdeen retain just 16 per cent of possession – it was clear that they needed to push further up the pitch, or it would merely be a matter of time before the Hoops extended their lead. Thelin relayed that message to his players at half-time, and within five minutes of the restart, Aberdeen had forced Kasper Schmeichel into an error, the Danish keeper kicking the ball straight out of play after some high pressure from Topi Keskinen and Nicky Devlin. From the resulting throw-in, Aberdeen won a free kick on the edge of the Celtic box. The early intent was promising.

The Red Army responded in kind, exploding into song as Clarkson stood over the ball.

Allez, allez, allez
Kings of all of Europe
Since 1983
Ferguson and Miller

The famous AFC
Red and white the colours
Of Scotland's finest team
We play at Pittodrie
The boys from Aberdeen

A hush fell as Leighton Clarkson stepped up to hit the free kick, and despite it coming to nothing, it felt like Aberdeen were starting to get a foothold in the match.

Hampden Park, 4.15pm

As the clock edged towards 60 minutes, Jimmy Thelin, after conversations with assistant Christer Persson and Peter Leven, decided that it was time for the first change of the game. Off came Topi Keskinen and on came the mercurial Pape Habib Guèye. The change allowed Aberdeen to go more direct with the ball and add much more of a physical and aerial presence to their ranks.

Guèye was jeered on to the pitch by the Celtic support – the Senegalese had been involved in a 50-50 tackle with Reo Hatate in the Pittodrie encounter two weeks prior, injuring the Celtic talisman and sidelining him for the final. Hatate, so often Celtic's difference-maker in the middle of the pitch, was clearly a huge loss for Rodgers's side. However, his absence was a boost for the Dons, and the supporters responded by cheering Guèye on to the pitch. Within a couple of minutes the substitute was making an impact, picking up the ball inside his own half and driving all the way up the pitch before winning a free kick outside the Celtic box. His efforts would be invaluable if Aberdeen were to restore parity.

Hampden Park, 4.25pm

There were now only 25 minutes remaining and Celtic were labouring, struggling to find the second goal that would put to bed any fears over an Aberdeen comeback. Arne Engels's low, curling strike looked like it had the pinpoint accuracy to beat Mitov but it instead clipped the outside of the post. An exhaling of relief could be felt from the west side of Hampden. Rodgers, becoming ever more agitated on the touchline, decided that he had seen enough. Adam Idah, Nicolas Kuhn and Arne Engels all made way to be replaced by James Forrest, Luke McCowan and Yang Hyun-jun. The replacement of the trio, who had a combined total of 83 goal involvements across the season, with three players who had contributed just 36, felt like a hasty move from Rodgers. The changes failed to make an instant impact. If anything, it was Aberdeen who benefited from Celtic's rhythm being disrupted, the Dons surging up field to win their first corner of the match minutes after the substitutions were made.

As former Aberdeen player Liam Scales sliced the ball behind, the fans, as one, roared in appreciation. Rory Hamilton was commentating on the game for broadcaster Premier Sports. 'The Celtic fans have a great reputation for making noise, but you could feel the nervousness or the sense that it might not be going their way,' said Hamilton. 'From the 70-minute mark onwards, you could feel something happening. With Pape Guèye coming on and giving Aberdeen something up top, it was important. It wasn't hurting Celtic yet, but it just meant that they weren't camped in their own box, and you could see the Aberdeen game plan taking shape. Where our commentary team sits, we are, of course, on the halfway line, so you are not influenced by being at one end or the other. There were more Celtic fans behind us, but you're getting a lot more of an even distribution of the noise, and by that stage of the game, undoubtedly, the noise was coming from my left-hand side from all of the Aberdeen fans.'

Hampden Park, 4.35pm

Ten minutes left. All of the fears of a heavy drubbing that the Aberdeen support had harboured before kick-off had failed to materialise. Sure, Celtic had dominated possession but had lacked the usual clinical edge that had seen them wipe the floor with so many teams over the course of the season. Their supporters tried to get behind their side and see them over the line to secure yet another domestic treble. Nobody had become more accustomed to losing to Celtic than Aberdeen fans – they had seen and heard it all before. In years gone by, they would be subject to the complete Celtic songbook, outnumbered in the stands and outgunned on the pitch. However, on this occasion, something felt different. Thelin's game plan had worked – with ten minutes to go, the Dons were within touching distance, and he decided that now was the time to strike. Just as Celtic had made a triple substitution, he made one of his own. Initially, Ante Palaversa's number went up on the fourth official's board, and the Croatian made his way off the pitch. However, Shayden Morris, Dante Polvara and Odday Dabbagh then replaced Leighton Clarkson, Kevin Nisbet and Alfie Dorrington. Amid the flurry of subs, Thelin suddenly realised that four players had come off the park and only three had gone on. Palaversa, who had already sat down on the bench, was called back to the touchline by his manager, who could be seen muttering 'fuck sake' under his breath on the TV cameras. Palaversa's name had been incorrectly noted down on the piece of paper handed to the fourth official, who had flashed his number up on the electronic board. With stress levels already at an all-time high the manager quickly looked to resolve the situation. After a quick consultation with the referee, Thelin got his midfield Croatian maestro back on to the pitch. It would prove a pivotal moment.

As if injected with a renewed zeal, it only took a few minutes for the substitutions to transform the game. Symptomatic of Celtic's sluggish second half, Paulo Bernardo gifted the ball to Guèye in the middle of the park. The gangling frame of the Senegalese lurched towards goal, harassed every step of the way by Celtic captain Callum McGregor. Guèye rode the challenge but was forced wide and out to the byline before cutting back and swinging the ball into the box. It came to nothing but was recycled by Morris. A few passes later, the ball ended up back with centre-half Milne. It was Aberdeen's first real moment of concerted pressure in the Celtic half, and the fans urged their team to come again, the anticipation building. Knoester popped the ball into the feet of Guèye, whose delicate touches took him away from the close attention of Alastair Johnston, and then past James Forrest into the middle of the pitch. He played the ball on to Palaversa, who in turn spotted Shayden Morris hugging the right-hand touchline. Knowing what the lightning-fast winger was capable of, an enormous cry of 'GO OOON!' rose in unison from the Dons fans as Morris received the ball. He took one touch, then another to get it out of his feet and whipped it into the corridor of uncertainty. A sudden silence fell over Hampden. The perfectly placed cross caused panic, and Schmeichel decided he would go to ground to deal with it. The Dane looked to scoop the ball away to safety but he had completely misjudged its flight, hitting him on the underside of his right arm. Instead of diverting the ball away from the goal, he had inexplicably turned it behind him and into the back of the net.

The mass of red behind the goal erupted. The guttural roar was so deafening it seemed to shake the very foundations of the stadium. It was utter bedlam as a sea of bodies, limbs flailing, jumped and bounced and completely lost themselves in the exhilaration of the moment. Sitting in the press box, with one of the best seats in the house to take it all in, was Michael Grant. 'The reaction to the equalising goal was just off the scale. I'll be honest – when the goal went in, I didn't write anything down. I just stood and watched. For about a minute, I didn't move. It was such a sight, such a visual thing. Absolute chaos. But there was something about that equaliser – it just sent a charge through the support.' As the chaos of the equaliser subsided, a thunderous, hair-raising chorus of 'Stand Free', that could be heard across the whole of the southside of Glasgow, was belted out. With only ten minutes of normal time remaining Aberdeen, from nowhere, were on level terms.

Hampden Park, 4.44pm

The next ten minutes were all about what was happening in the stands. The 2017 Scottish Cup Final had seen Aberdeen and Celtic locked at a goal apiece heading into the final five minutes, but this time was different. Aberdeen had just scored and the momentum was with them. The Red Army were absolutely determined to drag their team over the line.

Shady Mo
Shady Mo
Shady Mo
Shady Mo
Shady Mo, Mo, Mo
He is a winger
He came from Fleetwood
And his name is Shady Mo!

The support had never sounded so good as the travelling faithful serenaded their goalscorer. The bedrock of the noise was coming from the ultras, but it was intoxicating all around them. There were 20,000 fans singing every word of every song. It was off the scale. 'It's the Aberdeen fans who are making the noise here, Celtic look shaken by what's just happened,' declared Liam McLeod on commentary for BBC Scotland. A glance towards the East Stand would have told you that the Celtic supporters had become somewhat concerned, the majority of them suddenly chewing away at their fingernails. Their team wasn't doing much to alleviate their fears either; a string of misplaced passes and overhit crosses was met with jubilation in the Aberdeen end. Most impressively, Thelin's charges were not shrinking in the face of the occasion. After tracking right-back Johnston's run to the byline, Guèye shoulder-charged the Canadian, who collapsed in a heap such was the force of the challenge from the Senegalese spoiler. A roar of appreciation went up from the fans. As the ball trickled over the line, Maeda sprinted over to speed up the restart. Before he could get there, Guèye booted it as hard and as far away as he could – the prissy and obsequious Aberdeen that Celtic had walked all over at Hampden umpteen times before were unrecognisable. Aberdeen, on this day at least, were not there to be subjugated.

With minutes to go until full time, the Dons were defending with their lives as Celtic continued to seek a way through. And then, as the clock ticked into the 93rd minute, Maeda latched on to a break of the ball, his first touch taking him past the last Aberdeen defender and through on goal. Celtic's well-known penchant for late goals and drama, which had so often befallen Aberdeen, seemed poised to repeat itself. The spectre of Tom Rogic flashed high in the Hampden sky as fans watched the unfolding scene through their fingers. Not again, surely? But this time there was no lightning strike from the heavens. Dimitar Mitov hadn't read the script Celtic so craved and pulled off a stunning save when it mattered most – it was as good as a goal and celebrated as such by the Red Army. A late flurry of corners from Aberdeen, in which Milne blazed over the bar before the linesman's flag spared his blushes, added to the tension as the full-time whistle edged ever closer. One last push was needed from the fans and the Aberdeen rearguard as Celtic camped outside the box with the clock ticking towards the 97th minute. Milne, involved up the other end moments earlier, made a game-saving block as McGregor drilled in a low strike from the edge of the box. And that was it, full time. Aberdeen, against all of the odds, had taken the match into extra time.

Hampden Park, 4.55pm

As the players gathered around Thelin ahead of extra time, the fans, kicking every ball with their team, used the moment to take a short breather themselves. 'I was absolutely knackered, I was drained,' remembered Matt Findlay, the pre-match pints well and truly having worn off. 'It was such a muggy day, and the heat with everyone packed into that end was crazy. I went up to the kiosk to get a pint of water at full time. I was going up there and just wanted a moment to take a breather. I remember going into the toilet and someone said, "We're still in this, boys." It was like a team talk in the toilets!'

Hampden Park, 5pm

It was the third time in history that Aberdeen and Celtic had taken a Scottish Cup Final into extra time. In 1984, Mark McGhee struck in the added period to seal a third consecutive cup triumph for the Dons, edging a tense contest. Then came 1990 – the last time Aberdeen lifted the trophy, the drama stretching all the way to that famous penalty shoot-out. Crucially, Aberdeen had won on both occasions. However, that was 35 years ago, and this was the closest they had come to ending that long wait. It was at that point that some of the support truly started to believe that this could be their day. Omens were stacking up like signs from the football gods themselves. Brian Irvine, the penalty hero of 1990, was in the stands celebrating his 60th birthday. Out on the pitch, captain Graeme Shinnie was marking his 300th appearance in red. It was, so they said, the year of the underdog. Aberdeen's chequered kit for the season was a nod to the cup-winning strip of 1990. Celtic, meanwhile, looked strangely mortal, their usual swagger absent, and Daizen Maeda had already spurned a chance he would bury nine times out of ten – except today. Fate seemed to be circling overhead, whispering that Aberdeen's long suffering might finally be at an end. But there was no time to pause and listen for an answer from above – 30 more minutes lay ahead, 30 minutes to seize the cup. The vocal cords fired up one more.

Hampden Park, 5.15pm

The first half of extra time was a non-event as both teams tired and continued to shuffle the pack. James Forrest came off injured for Celtic, while Milne, who had put in the performance of his life and had nothing left to give, was replaced by Latvian Kristers Tobers. Celtic continued to dominate the ball but Aberdeen were relentless and dogged in their defending. The fans continued to drive their team on – the backing was unbelievable. When Celtic had the ball, a corner or a threatening situation, there was no lull in the singing – the support repudiated that this would not be their day. The television cameras panned over to the Dons fans frequently, and, on every occasion, every section on the west side of Hampden was bouncing. After the first 15 minutes of extra time had elapsed, the Aberdeen players quickly gathered around their manager for final words. The Swede, usually so calm and collected, looked the most animated he had been all season as he offered some last words of encouragement and advice – the passion, for the first time, was written all over his face.

Hampden Park, 5.20pm

On commentary, it was said that the best opportunity for Aberdeen to win the trophy was on penalties – it certainly didn't look like that. Straight from kick-off Aberdeen were on the attack, and Morris, who was causing Celtic all sorts of problems, won yet another corner. The ball was swung in and nodded down inside the box by Guèye. Dante Polvara swung his foot and struck sweetly on the volley – his effort whistled inches over the bar. The entire Dons end put their hands on their heads as one, as if choreographed; was that the golden opportunity? The tension was unbearable. 'It felt like my heart was going to pop out of my chest,' said fan Ryan Alexander, who was watching from behind the goal. 'We had been standing the whole game, so my legs felt as if I had been out on the pitch myself. Every attack at either end was almost unbearable. The heat I remember was so oppressive that it felt difficult to breathe at times. This was the most important 15 minutes in the club's recent history. You could feel that tension, but everyone just kept on singing.' The second period of extra time was end-to-end. Jeffrey Schlupp struck the bar before Guèye scuffed a shot into the ground on the breakaway, making it easy for Schmeichel to gather. The game entered its final five minutes. This was it. Aberdeen had just five minutes to hold out to get to penalties. The Red Army, if it was even possible, took their support to another level over the final moments.

Come on you Reds
Come on you Reds
Come on you Reds

Two minutes to full time. Celtic were penning Aberdeen in now as they searched for the late goal, but there was no way through. One minute to go. The treble chasers worked the ball out wide to Johnston, who punched in a cross deep to the back post. Maeda got their first and helped it back into the six-yard box where Carter-Vickers was waiting. Aberdeen hearts were in mouths, helplessly watching the action unfold up the other end. The towering American got his head to the ball but it was too high to get any purchase on, and his effort looped up into the air. Mitov jumped high into the Hampden sky to collect and fell to the ground with the ball safely in his arms. A thunderous roar went up from the Aberdeen fans and the referee blew his whistle. That was it. Just as it was 35 years ago, it was spot-kicks standing between Aberdeen and the Scottish Cup.

Hampden Park, 5.25pm

As the players walked off the pitch to prepare for penalties, the stadium tannoy blared out 'All These Things That I've Done' by the Killers.

The battle is won
With all these things that I've done
If you can hold on
If you can hold on

The song itself is about growing up and moving on from the past – it felt like a subtle yet significant moment. The Aberdeen players gathered round in a group as they worked out their penalty takers. Kevin Nisbet, substituted after 80 minutes, took on the role of one of the coaching staff, buzzing about asking who was keen to take a penalty and helping his manager write down the order in which they would step up. The list was finalised, and it was time for final words. Shinnie gathered everyone round to tell them that, whatever happened, he was mightily proud of them and their efforts – they had left absolutely everything out on the pitch. Everyone had expected Aberdeen to turn up and be steamrollered by the Celtic juggernaut. That hadn't transpired, and the pressure was all on the Hoops to try and salvage their treble hopes.

Adam Rooney became a hero for the club when he scored the winning penalty in the 2014 League Cup Final – 11 years on, he was in the stands for this shoot-out. 'It was brilliant being in the crowd and seeing the other side of it. I thought in the second half, Aberdeen did very well, and it was a great game from half-time onwards. It was great to have my son there; he was getting as excited as the rest of the Aberdeen fans, bouncing up and down and singing along when it got to penalties.' Rooney, something of a penalty specialist himself during his time at Pittodrie, scored 20 of his 22 penalties in an Aberdeen shirt. 'The boys would have been practising penalties all week, just in case it came to that scenario. Ahead of cup finals in my time at Aberdeen, at the end of every training session that week, you would have to walk from the halfway line and take a penalty and walk back. It's completely different once you are in the moment, of course. You have to blank out all of the noise and focus on making decent contact with the ball. When you see the ball hit the net, it's a total relief. The only penalties that I missed were when I was indecisive and doubted myself on the day, and maybe changed my mind. You just can't do that and have to stick with what you have practised.'

Hampden Park, 5.30pm

As the captains came together to speak to referee Don Robertson, it was Callum McGregor who won the toss on both occasions. Celtic would take the first penalty in front of their own fans. In fact, it was McGregor himself who had decided that he was going to take the first spot-kick of the shoot-out. The hopes of the entirety of the north-east of Scotland lay in the gloves of Dimitar Mitov. The Bulgarian had already saved two penalties over the course of the season – both in games the Dons had gone on to win. This was different; however, this was the Scottish Cup Final. Joe Lewis was waiting and watching on from afar. 'I had an event planned, which I couldn't get out of, which meant I couldn't get to the game. I was gutted to be missing it. So, I was watching it on my phone, nervous as anyone. As a goalkeeper in a penalty shoot-out, you have the opportunity to be the match winner and win the trophy. It's a rare thing for a goalkeeper. I used to wish extra time away when I was in goals as I wanted to save some penalties – most goalkeepers are the same, and Mitov would have gained a lot of confidence from his last-minute save from Maeda.'

McGregor stepped up to a ringing of boos and whistles from the Aberdeen fans, determined to do anything they could to make the Celtic captain feel as nervous as possible despite being 300 yards away. The Bulgarian shot-stopper more than had it covered, though, throwing himself to his right, getting two strong hands to push the ball away. He immediately leapt to his feet, pointing to the sky. It was a monumental save. McGregor, head in hands, couldn't believe it. It was advantage Aberdeen.

Dons captain Graeme Shinnie was his team's first penalty taker. He had spoken countless times about how he had regretted not taking a penalty in the 2014 League Cup Final for Inverness Caledonian Thistle and vowed he would never shirk the responsibility again. It had been an incredible performance from Shinnie over the 120 minutes in the middle of the pitch. The doubters who had said his legs were gone had been silenced for at least another day. Left-footed, Shinnie stepped on to his penalty with conviction and fired it right into the top corner. It was the perfect start. He jogged back to join his team-mates on the halfway line, pointing towards the badge upon his chest as he did so. Thelin puffed out his cheeks on the touchline. Aberdeen were four penalties away from glory.

Celtic got their shoot-out off the mark when Johnny Kenny, on as a substitute, coolly sent Mitov one way and then the ball the other. Fans' favourite Dante Polvara was next up for the Dons. He steadied himself at the edge of the box, closing his eyes to take a deep breath. A stutter run-up added to the drama before he fired the ball into the bottom corner. Relief. Just as Shinnie had done, the American clutched at the badge on his shirt as he celebrated. Luke McCowan was next for Celtic, keen to waste no time, his short run-up deceiving Mitov and the former Dundee man dispatching the ball into the back of the net to level. 'I'd covered the cup final in 2020 – the Covid final – when Celtic beat Hearts on penalties,' recalled Michael Grant, who was kicking every ball in the press box. 'Hearts were actually leading in that shoot-out; the cup was in their hands, and they blew it. Two in a row they didn't score, and Celtic went on to win. That game was in my head all through this shoot-out. I've seen Celtic so many times come through, even when they don't play well – they always seem to win in the end. So, when our players were stepping up, I feared every single one of them would miss. But the penalties … They were majestic. You could have set them to music.'

Semi-final hero Oday Dabbagh continued the streak of stunning penalties for Aberdeen, sending his strike, once again, into the top corner – it was quite astonishing. The bench exploded. Jimmy Thelin gave a double fist-pump when the ball hit the net, while behind him Kevin Nisbet, still with his substitute's bib on, went mental. He then pulled the bib up and over his head, unable to contain his nerves. The supporters couldn't believe what they were watching. Their team was now only two penalties away. As Dabbagh passed Maeda, walking up to take the next kick, the Palestinian shouted something at the Celtic talisman in an attempt to put him off. It almost worked. Maeda nonchalantly blasted his penalty down the middle of the goal, which Mitov anticipated, but the shot slipped through his gloves and into the net. Ante Palaversa stepped forward with all of the confidence and purpose that you would expect of a Croat. His penalty arced away and out of the reach of Schmeichel, helpless to stop it from hitting the back of the net. Palaversa immediately turned and cupped his ears to the dejected Celtic support, who were witnessing their treble dream crumble before their eyes. The pressure was on now, and Brendan Rodgers's team had to score the subsequent penalty or, remarkably, it would be Aberdeen's cup. The responsibility fell to full-back Alastair Johnston. As the Canadian made the long walk from the halfway line, he knew what was at stake. Mitov knew it too. Johnston's kick was angled low and left, and, just as he had done for the first penalty, Mitov sprang to his right. Hampden held its breath. SAVED.

Hampden Park, 5.50pm

Aberdeen, after 35 years, were Scottish Cup champions once more.

11

At Last

AS DIMITAR Mitov dived to his right and pushed Alastair Johnston's penalty away, the rows of red on the west side of Hampden disappeared and were replaced by one shuddering mass of euphoric humanity. Thirty-five years of hoping, heartbreak and dreaming came flooding out in one explosive release. In that moment the heavy curtain of gloom fell away, and spectres of previous Scottish Cup traumas vanquished. None of it mattered anymore. The Red Army was a red wall, and, in that moment, they felt 100ft tall. If this were Hollywood, Etta James's 'At Last' would be set as the overture to the scenes unfolding on and off the pitch. A glance at any section of the Aberdeen support represented a live-action renaissance painting – tears fell, hands clutched heads in disbelief, family, friends and strangers alike collapsed into each other's arms. Delirium gripped and shook those in red to the core.

> Michael Grant: 'Everyone was in tears as you looked around. For young ones, it was the first time they'd ever seen us lift the Scottish Cup. For the older ones, it was just as emotional. I'm now

56, and I was 21 the last time we won the cup. It was unthinkable that we would have to wait 35 years for it again. And of course, over those 35 years, you lose people: family members, your mum and dad, friends that you were at the final with the last time, or that you've been to games with and that have passed away. So, regardless of what age you were, it was emotional. You only get that when you have had to wait decades for something.'

The outpouring of emotion unfolding was of an unprecedented scale. You would have struggled to find a dry eye in the house over those intoxicating couple of minutes. Although they bounced and moved as one mass, every one of the 20,000 Aberdeen fans wore their own story on their faces.

Michael Duncan: 'In December 2023, my dad was diagnosed with cancer. As it does for every family, it turned our world upside down. Football is a family affair for us – I enjoy going to matches with my mates, but unless my dad and my brother are there with me, it's not the same. We came away from Hampden after the 1-0 League Cup Final defeat to Rangers thinking this might be our last cup final together. Thankfully, my dad officially beat cancer in early 2025, and the three of us, me, my dad and brother, all made it to Hampden again on 24 May. When Mitov saved that final penalty, we were all hugging each other tight and absolutely bawling our eyes out.'

Darren Abel: 'I have been taking my nephew Nath to football with me since he was five years old, and we have talked about a day like 24 May 2025, as we travelled up and down the country following the Dons, for as long as I can remember. The entire day was amazing; photos with flags before we left, discussing how it was going to go travelling down, both looking for the slightest bit of hope to cling on to. We have always been close, and when Nath lost his dad in 2023, the bond became even stronger. It's not going to be long until Nath wants to go and get drunk, and enjoy the football with his pals, just like I did. We will always have that moment now, and I'm not scared to admit that when Mitov saved that penalty, holding each other, tears of joy running down our cheeks, it is one of the best moments of my life.'

Duncan Milne: 'I was 17 when we won the cup in 1990. As I left Hampden that day, I thought we'd be back every few years. If only I'd known what was coming in the years ahead. After the 6-0 League Cup semi-final, I said I'd never go back to Hampden. The drubbing, the rubbish stadium, and the nightmare getting to and from Glasgow put me off. A Scottish Cup Final got me back. When the final penalty was saved, I didn't know what to do at that moment. There was lots of hugging and tears. Throughout the day my thoughts drifted to two Dons fans who weren't there – one who I'd stood with in 1990 was now living Down Under, and another who sadly passed away in 2003 and never saw us win a cup in the flesh. Nothing will ever come close to matching this cup win.'

Glen Schreuder: 'This was my five-year-old son's first cup final. He had been to every home game in our run to the final, similar to the season before, and had only ever seen victories. I felt compelled to take him with me for this one, hoping to maintain our good luck. The night before, he drew a poster of Oday Dabbagh and was so excited he wanted to sleep in his Aberdeen kit. Throughout the game, he stood on his chair, singing and shouting, though he did need a few short rests. It was the most engaged I've ever seen him. Booing McGregor as he walked up to take his penalty, cheering the miss, cheering each Aberdeen goal. The sheer elation as he jumped into my arms when Mitov saved from Johnston was amazing – those moments will stay with me for ever as we bounced up and down amid the swirling bodies around us. Tears, smiles, disbelief! It all made it worthwhile! What a day, what a moment!'

As the Red Army collectively unleashed 35 years of pent-up frustration, lifelong dreams suddenly realised, the on-pitch scenes were every bit as good as the ones in the stands. Not that the Aberdeen support inside Hampden would have noticed, but there was actually a very brief VAR check to see whether Mitov was off his line as he saved the final penalty. The Aberdeen players were rushing towards Mitov in jubilation, but, as they did so, their goalkeeper was telling them to keep a lid on the celebrations. The referee then blew his whistle, confirming that the cup was Aberdeen's. Mitov was mobbed by his team-mates, including those who hadn't made the matchday squad, kitted out in their suits, all of them bouncing up and down, grabbing everyone and everything in sight.

Back at the halfway line, when Mitov had made the save, captain Graeme Shinnie sank to his knees, arms outstretched to the heavens. This was his day of reckoning. On his 300th appearance for his hometown club, he would lift the Scottish Cup. Fate. The footballing gods had answered his prayers. Shinnie collapsed, sobbing into the turf, emotionally spent. His team-mates, celebrating up at the east end of Hampden where the penalty shoot-out had taken place, collectively realised they were doing so away from the Aberdeen support and ran towards the heaving red sea in the west. The players were welcomed as heroes as they reached the Aberdeen end, some of them knee-sliding in their elation, including Jamie McGrath, in his suit. It was a surreal scene. In the backdrop, as Celtic fans were flooding out of the stadium, the big screen at Hampden flashed up 'Congratulations Aberdeen' in red and white.

For Dons fans who had become conditioned to Hampden heartache, it felt as if they had been dropped into an alternative reality – this kind of thing didn't happen. As the initial explosion subsided, the supporters pulled themselves out of the clutches of one another and came together as a single entity. A victorious cry of 'Stand Free', the first at the national stadium this century, reverberated around the ground. At that exact moment, BBC Radio Scotland grabbed Ante Palaversa for some immediate reaction.

With the deafening noise in the background, the Croatian, the adrenaline surging through him, shouted down the microphone on national radio, 'This is fucking amazing, this is fucking history.' He was not wrong. Even the stoic Willie Miller, in the stands covering the game for the radio, admitted to feeling a bit 'unsettled' given the enormity of what was unfolding.

After somewhat composing himself, Shinnie, tears of joy still welling in his eyes, bounded over to join the celebrations, pumping his fists towards the crowd and thumping the Aberdeen badge on his chest. A roar of recognition went up for the man who had suffered through most of the recent Scottish Cup disappointments along with the fans. 'Graeme Shinnie, he's one of our own,' sang the fans, who still couldn't quite believe what they were seeing.

As for the man who had masterminded the win, Jimmy Thelin celebrated in a huddle with his coaching staff and assistant Christer Persson, who had been by his side since his first managerial appointment at Jönköping-Södra – it had been a monumental journey. And now, in his first season at Aberdeen, he had brought glory to the Granite City once more. The Swede had already cemented himself as a legend at the club for ever. A measure of the man, he peeled himself away from the celebrations and took a moment to shake hands with Brendan Rodgers before doing the same with the disconsolate Celtic players. He then joined the celebrations, darting between his heroes, congratulating them in turn, a smile as broad as the North Sea splashed across his face. All season long, Thelin had spoken about how the togetherness between the players and fans could deliver something special. And together, on this day of all days, they had.

Stewart Smith: 'When Mitov saved that penalty, nothing else in the world mattered but celebrating with my cousins and the rest of the best fanbase I have ever been a part of. It was unbelievable. I cried my eyes out, then composed myself, only for the tears to flow again when my dad, who was in the Isle of Man and couldn't make the game, called me as "The Northern Lights of Old Aberdeen" was being sung. He's the reason I'm an Aberdeen fan. As the players celebrated with the fans, I realised my train was becoming very tight, but I couldn't miss the trophy-lift. So, before it happened, I said my goodbyes to my cousins and let them know I'd be off as soon as the cup was lifted.'

Kathleen Gray: 'My son Matthew, who is 17 and has ADHD and autism, went to the Scottish Cup Final with his granda and came home saying he'd made memories he'll never forget. It was Matthew's first cup final, and he was so glad to share it with his granda, who, at nearly 80, says it might be his last. The experience has forged a special bond between them, carrying on a family tradition that began when I went to games with my own granda. Matthew now loves reminding me that he was there and I wasn't. I couldn't face another final after so many defeats, but I'm delighted he'll have these memories for life – stories to cherish long after his granda is gone.'

Aberdeen. Scottish Cup winners. For years, it had seemed like an impossible dream, slipping further out of reach with every passing season. But now, against all expectations, it was a reality. Finally, the supporters were going to see their team walk up the fabled Hampden steps to lift the trophy once more. 'As the game was wearing on, especially after Aberdeen equalised, me and Michael [Stewart] turned to each other on the gantry and said, "Aberdeen are going to win this on penalties,"' said Rory Hamilton, commentating on the game for Premier Sports. 'It almost starts to become written in the stars when you think back to how it happened in 1990. That was the logical conclusion to Aberdeen's wait for the trophy. You can't prepare for what you are going to say during a game, but you can for the things you know will happen. I had a few lines written for the trophy-lift should it have been either team.'

Hamilton's description of the moment the fans had craved for decades will go down in history: 'The Aberdeen skipper looks in disbelief. The moment of anticipation is almost over, as Graeme Shinnie gets his hands on the trophy. The 2025 Scottish Cup winners are Aberdeen! And the Scottish Cup will sparkle at Pittodrie once again. They dared to dream and dream big. Not many gave them a chance today, but they believed, they delivered and three decades of the weight of success are released. From Alex Miller, Theo Snelders and Brian Irvine in 1990. From Sir Alex Ferguson, John Hewitt, Billy Stark, Black, McGhee, Strachan, Miller, McLeish, Cooper, Harper, McKay, Hamilton, Williams, Halliday to Eddie Turnbull. These were the Scottish Cup heroes of yesteryear. For this season, read the names Mitov, Devlin, Shinnie, Knoester, Nisbet, Clarkson, Palaversa, Milne, Dorrington, Jensen, Keskinen, Doohan, MacKenzie, Polvara, Dabbagh, Guèye, Morris, Tobers, and Boyd. The full squad, led by Jimmy Thelin, who has delivered the almighty prize for the Dons. What they have craved for 35 long, long years. For Aberdeen, the trophy is coming home to the Granite City, to the north-east, where they held it for so long in the glory years; this is the glory day for Aberdeen. They are the 2025 Scottish Cup winners.'

Just like Willie Miller in the 1980s, the image of Shinnie clutching the Scottish Cup, adorned in red and white ribbons, in one hand, both arms outstretched, will go down in Aberdeen folklore for eternity. As will all of the players who finally made it happen. For Oday Dabbagh, however fleeting his stint, his contributions had been instrumental in the success. The Palestinian international had only scored four goals during his four months at the club following his deadline-day arrival in February. However, his two quarter-final goals, last-minute semi-final heroics against Hearts, and sensational cup final penalty offered comparisons to Aberdeen's famous 'Cup-Tie' McKay, who had sped the Dons on the way to their 1970 Scottish Cup success. Football is quite remarkable in that a boy who grew up playing football on the streets of Jerusalem, one day hoping to become a professional player, will now be remembered for ever as a hero in the north-east of Scotland. Winning the Scottish Cup would not have been possible without Dabbagh.

Watching the trophy-lift in the stands, his delight uncontrollable, was one of those very heroes from yesteryear. 'Seeing the players down on the pitch celebrating and then lifting the trophy brought back all of the memories from 1990,' said Brian Irvine. 'It was so refreshing to be able to enjoy some new memories after all of these years. The Aberdeen fans were incredible on the day, and it was great that they managed to get that 50-50 split of tickets. I thought it was a really poignant sight at the end when all of the Celtic fans had left, and it was just the Aberdeen supporters left inside Hampden. It was our day. It was such a wonderful experience for the players and the fans on the day. It certainly wasn't about me, but it was just so nice everything seemed to align. We had an event at the Aberdeen Music Hall leading up to the cup final, celebrating the 35 years since the last win. A couple of days later, it's my 60th birthday, and I'm heading down to the game. It's brilliant that there's going to be someone else to be able to speak about their glory in the 2025 cup final, rather than bringing out Brian Irvine from the age of the dinosaurs. It will be somebody more relevant now.'

And that was why it meant so much. Finally, after years of hurt and ridicule, the Aberdeen fans now had new heroes, new legends, and new memories made in the company of those who meant most.

Malcolm Crombie: 'It's difficult to put into words what that day was like. I was there in 1990 when we won the last Scottish Cup, I was there in Gothenburg in 1983 when we won the European Cup Winners' Cup, I was there in 1984 when we beat Celtic to win the Scottish Cup three years in a row, but 2025 is the one that will sit proudest in the memory. The best day of my life sounds like an exaggeration, but I can't remember another day so glorious that I got to share with my family and friends. The only person missing, my dad, who started me out on this love affair with Aberdeen Football Club. But we had cups galore back in the 80s to enjoy together, we had Gothenburg together, this moment was for the next generation of Aberdeen fans – those like my son born in 1997, who has travelled far and wide supporting the Dons. With the exception of the League Cup in 2014, it's usually been a path that ultimately leads to failure and us questioning "why do we do it?"; 24 May 2025 was why we do it and why we always go back. For the generation of Dandies born after 1983, this was their Gothenburg. And somewhere up above, my dad was watching on, with a big toothy grin on his face.'

Richard Caldicott: 'For me, the final was all about sharing it with my 18-year-old old son. He'd seen us lose twice at Hampden to Rangers in the last two years, seen us battered by Celtic at Hampden – he even saw Curtis Main destroy us for Motherwell at Hampden! He cried when Tom Rogic scored in 2017 – he was ten and it was last time I saw him cry. However, this time at the final whistle my son put his head on my chest and cried for ten minutes straight. Absolute tears of happiness. This one was for him.'

Gus Tawse: 'Aberdeen have been my team since childhood, though I rarely went to Pittodrie early on. Playing juvenile football on Saturdays meant games were a treat, then adult life, work and family pushed football aside. I was the kind of fan who turned up only for semis and finals. That changed in 2023. The Scottish Cup semi-final against Celtic, despite defeat, convinced me to buy my first season ticket. Soon, I was swept up in the buzz of Jimmy's reign, travelling to away games. Most welcomed me, and friendships grew – including one that became life-changing. A first date at Rugby Park led to love, moving in together, and following the Dons side by side. Cup final week was filled with dread and hope. When Mitov saved for the second time and we were confirmed as Scottish Cup winners for the first time in 35 years, I hugged my partner and didn't want to let go. This was truly one of the greatest days of my life and I had someone special to share it with.'

Gilbert Falconer: 'The cup final win was special to me for a variety of reasons. It was the first Scottish Cup Final where I had my daughter and granddaughter with me. My first Scottish Cup Final was in 1970, and I wore a replica shirt of that win under my shirt and tie. I was commentating for blind fans from the media section, so I had dressed in a businesslike fashion. My daughter had been too young to attend our last Scottish Cup Final win, so she was used to our more recent disappointments in the competition. It was surreal to be commentating on the penalties after extra time, as I doubted if the blind guys were hearing me due to the batteries possibly running out in their receivers, but I kept at it nonetheless! The support from the Dons fans was outstanding, and the opposition fans were hardly heard throughout. After the trophy presentation, I made my way to the car park to retrieve the sets from my blind friends, and the delirium was infectious, to say the least. My daughter and granddaughter had both burst into tears of joy at the end, and it was an experience that will live in our memories as long as we live.'

On the Hampden pitch, a temporary stage was assembled for the presentation. Aberdeen's entire squad – including those not involved on the day – along with the coaching staff, joined together for the trophy-lift. When Graeme Shinnie raised the Scottish Cup aloft, gold confetti filled the air, flames erupted and the Red Army responded with another deafening roar. The trophy was then passed between players for photographs, each taking a moment to savour the occasion. As Jack MacKenzie got his hands on it, Dante Polvara dragged the defender in front of the fans, ensuring that he got an extra special reception given the events that had transpired at Tannadice just a week prior. MacKenzie was headed south at the end of the season, the Scottish Cup Final being his last game for the club. It ended in the best conceivable way.

When the trophy reached the man who had made everyone believe, Jimmy Thelin immediately turned towards the supporters. He lifted the cup high, pointed first to the silverware and then to the stands, making clear where the credit lay. It was a simple gesture but one that underlined the bond he had built with supporters over the season – a reminder that, in his eyes, this victory was theirs as much as his. He couldn't hide his delight in his post-match press conference: 'I think you hear with our supporters today and their faces [what this means]. The smile on the city, the players and the staff. All this week we have tried to visualise how we can win this game and create this belief. The way the players compete today out there, I am so proud how they used the energy from our supporters who travelled down here. What can I say, I'm happy, relieved, tired and I am going to enjoy this evening! I have quite a lot of emotions right now, I have to say. I am also so proud because my family is back in Sweden, my wife and my kids. They have allowed me to do this journey, and they have been so supportive all of the time. My brother was here today. I have called them already. My parents, my wife's parents and everybody was in our house back in Sweden and watched the game together and they were so happy.'

Thelin had not only delighted the supporters but also his chairman, whose support never wavered even during the difficult winter. 'I went on to the pitch at the end, initially I was in two minds about it, but others encouraged me,' explained Dave Cormack. 'I wanted to thank Jimmy and Graeme [Shinnie]; I know Graeme very well, as I used to play football with his dad, and he went to the same school as my wife and sister-in-law. Aberdeen is a small place, you know. But for me, I was drawn throughout the game to watching the fans. Seeing them all there with smiles on their faces at the end was great. That was a truly incredible Hampden experience, the best I've ever witnessed, and I've been to a lot of finals.'

Of course, despite the best efforts of Cormack to secure as many tickets for the fans as possible, not everyone could make it to Hampden for the occasion. To those watching on in their homes or from afar, it meant just as much.

Roderick Murray: 'My son Stuart was born in 1984 and grew up during Aberdeen's golden era. From an early age he was captivated by football, replaying Gothenburg videos and coming with me to Pittodrie, where we both held season tickets. We travelled to pre-season games in the Highlands, camped overnight, and took in countless away days together. He was even a mascot against Rangers in 1990. In his lifetime he only saw Aberdeen win one trophy in person – the 1995 League Cup Final against Dundee – as he was considered too young for earlier trips to Hampden. Stuart died in a car accident in 2005, but I have carried his memory into every match since. When Dimi Mitov's penalty save sealed the Scottish Cup, I was at home shouting and dancing in the living room. Messages from Stuart's friends soon followed, reminding me how much joy my son would have felt – and why this triumph meant so much.'

Brian Sloan: 'Our family is facing unimaginable challenges at the moment – my wife, just 44, has been diagnosed with early onset Alzheimer's, and, with two young children, life has taken a very difficult turn. Moments of real joy have become rare. But on Scottish Cup Final day, those challenges paused, if only briefly. Under Jimmy's leadership, Aberdeen gave me the happiest day I've had since my wife's diagnosis. For 90 minutes and beyond, I felt something I hadn't in a long time: pure happiness. I smiled, I celebrated, I cried, and for a while the weight I carry lifted. This victory was more than a trophy. The team's passion, composure and unity restored pride and belief, not just in the support, but in me personally. For that day at least, I felt alive again.'

In the half an hour following the trophy-lift, the fans basked in the emotions that they had sought for 35 years. Exalted joy was on the face of every single supporter. The players, still careering about the pitch with the trophy in hand, continued to lift the famous piece of silverware aloft triumphantly to the supporters – every single time it was met with an enormous cheer. Back in Aberdeen, the celebrations were already in full swing. The Foundry Bar was bouncing. 'Wow, when Mitov saved that penalty the roof nearly came off the building,' said deputy manager Kieren Joseph. 'That night, by 8pm we were full to capacity, and the atmosphere was electric. Every song was changed to the Aberdeen football version, and it truly was amazing to see the fans celebrate like they did.' It would be a party that would go on long into the summer.

At Hampden, as the carnival atmosphere was drawing to a close, you could see fans looking around, once again in disbelief, trying to burn every single thing they were seeing into their minds for eternity. In the 80s, many thought that the good times would continue to roll and that there would be no let-up of red-and-white dominance in Scottish football. With the benefit of hindsight, the supporters at Hampden ensured that they savoured every second of this historic day. For the generation raised on stories of legendary European trophies and domestic dominance, Saturday, 24 May 2025 was their Gothenburg. Even for those who were at the Ullevi that famous night to see Aberdeen topple the great Real Madrid, this cup win rivals it – including for Dave Cormack. 'For me, being in Gothenburg was an incredible experience,' said the chairman. 'It was a time when Aberdeen and Dundee United were doing really well in Scotland and in Europe. Having beaten Bayern Munich, there was real optimism we could beat Real Madrid, because back then you didn't have the game-changing television money in the top five leagues dominating the landscape financially. And so, the fact it was 35 years on from the last Scottish Cup win, the fact we were underdogs, and the supporters getting together to create not just an incredible display in red, but getting together to get behind the team for the whole 90, which turned out to be 120 minutes, I was really just so pleased for the city and all of our supporters. It had been a long time coming, and it was a huge release of emotion. Obviously, winning the European Cup Winners' Cup versus the Scottish Cup is at a different level but, given where we are today, with the money that is in football, for me that is why this is right up there with Gothenburg.'

As the players headed up the tunnel, with the Scottish Cup in tow, the national stadium began to empty, the Red Army dispersing, taking with them their jubilation into the Glasgow night.

> Ryan Alexander: 'The pure joy exiting Hampden after the match among 20,000 Dandies was intoxicating. Wandering the streets around Mount Florida, drinking beer, singing, hugging, shaking each other that it really happened. This was why we kept going back, even when the odds seemed stacked against us. When the train back from Mount Florida pulled into Central Station and a sea of red and white filed out with a triumphant chorus of "Stand Free", which almost took the

roof off, that was when it truly started to sink in. We had done it, we were there, the cup was ours, and Glasgow belonged to us that Saturday night.'

Everywhere you looked in Glasgow city centre – on street corners, in pubs, spilling out into the streets – there were Aberdeen fans. Strangers in red greeted each other like old friends, as if reunited after years apart. As the Red Army partied long into the night, the news broke that the victory parade would be held the following day at noon, back in the Granite City. For one day at least, Celtic and Glasgow had been conquered. Now it was time to head back north. For the first time in 35 years, the Scottish Cup was coming home.

12

Granite Gratification

ABERDEEN HAS always been different. Perched on the edge of the North Sea, two and a half hours from the central belt by road or rail, it sits apart from the rest of Scotland. Even in ancient times, the north-east stood alone. Long before the formation of what we now know as modern-day Scotland, this was the land of the Picts, a reticent people who spoke an undecipherable language and carved their mysterious stones into the landscape. They left behind a heritage that marked them as disparate from the other kingdoms in northern Britain at the time – their customs and symbols never truly understood. Centuries may have passed, but it is still true to this day that Aberdonians regard themselves as distinct from the rest of Scotland both culturally and geographically. This isolation has, over hundreds of years, instilled a self-sufficient mentality among the people of the north-east of Scotland.

In modern footballing terms, the difference has only sharpened. Across Scotland's four largest cities, three of them find themselves divided. In Glasgow there's Celtic and Rangers. In Edinburgh, Hibernian and Heart of Midlothian. In Dundee, straddling opposite sides of the same road, sit Dundee and Dundee United. Only in Aberdeen does the whole city stand behind one club. In truth, the club's influence reaches much further afield than the city boundaries, stretching out far into Aberdeenshire, given that it is the only top-flight club within a 60-mile radius. Aberdeen Football Club is an institution of the north-east and, unlike any of the other top clubs in Scotland, it represents an entire region rather than a particular section of society. In that sense it can be viewed in a similar way to that of Athletic Club from the Basque region in Spain.

Primarily concentrated along the western fringe of the Pyrenees in Spain's north-east, the Basques consider themselves a nation within a nation – ethnically and culturally distinct from the rest of the country. Basques denounce the influence of the Castilian majority, especially those from Madrid, existing as a bastion of independent identity. As such, matches against teams from outside of northern Spain, particularly Real Madrid, can be passionate, hostile affairs as Basques seek to remind everyone of the strength of their distinct identity. In Aberdeen, the parallels are clear. Most of Scotland's population resides in the central belt, and its residents often dismiss the north-east as some grim, peripheral outpost. Aberdeen, to outsiders, is remote, rural, cold, dour – locals get called 'sheepshaggers' and teased for their accent and the Doric dialect, a distinctive element of the region's culture.

Things only became more polarised during the 1980s as cultural and economic landscapes began to shift. Aberdeen became the oil capital of Europe and experienced unprecedented levels of prosperity, while the rest of the country underwent economic hardships as a result of the manufacturing industries suffering a heavy decline. The changing fortunes were mirrored on the pitch. Aberdeen, under Alex Ferguson, broke the stranglehold of the Glasgow duopoly on the Scottish game, and established themselves as Scotland's top dogs. Indeed, they were ranked as the world's best side for the vast majority of 1984 – it was something the rest of Scottish football, particularly those in Glasgow, found difficult to accept. Although times have once again changed since the turn of the millennium, the sense of identity and belonging to the area has never dwindled among those in Aberdeen and the shire, who remain fiercely proud of their heritage. Just as it has for centuries, the feeling that life is different in the north-east of Scotland perseveres – evident in the fact that the club's motto is *Stand Free*. Even though far removed from the rest of Scottish football, Aberdeen's one-club city status is one of its greatest attributes. In a way that is not possible in Glasgow or Edinburgh, when the football club achieves success, the whole city comes out to celebrate – none more so than the 2025 Scottish Cup victory parade.

The celebrations went long into the early hours of the following day as Aberdeen revelled in one of the most famous victories in their history. After their Hampden heroics, the players and coaching staff hopped back on board the team bus, the Scottish Cup taking pride of place on the dashboard, and partied all the way back up the road. At Pittodrie, the chairman was waiting to meet them. 'We got back up to Aberdeen and then went to Pittodrie,' said Dave Cormack. 'We had some of the staff there, as well as the players, some of their families, and obviously the coaching staff, Jimmy and the guys. I think everybody was pretty exhausted. I'm an old boy now, right? So, I went for about 45 minutes or an hour, because we knew the next day was going to start fairly quickly. It was great to get back up there and actually have a little bit of time with the families. Everyone was obviously delighted but exhausted. I think I got to bed at about one in the morning.'

There was a fair chance that Cormack was the first person in bed across the whole of Aberdeen that night, some no doubt deciding against sleep entirely as the celebrations rolled on into the night. That included the players themselves, some of them hitting the town along with the supporters. If there was anyone nursing a hangover the next day then the perfect tonic was the first Scottish Cup trophy parade the city had seen in 35 years. Granted, the midday start was a quick turnaround, but the city had waited three and a half decades for this moment; it could barely wait an extra hour. Trophy parades in the Granite City are always momentous occasions, and for the players lucky enough to have experienced them in their time at the club, they attest to the special scenes that they generate. 'I vividly remember coming up Union Street with people everywhere, waving their flags and cheering,' said Brian Irvine, the hero of 1990. 'Waving the cup to the supporters below you from the Town House is a moment that will for ever stay with me. I can still hear them cheering!'

All of the great teams and club legends had enjoyed the hero's return to Aberdeen, and now, a similar welcome awaited the class of 2025. The squad, most of them with beverages in hand and sunglasses covering their eyes, hopped on board the special red bus, boasting 'Scottish Cup Winners' emblazoned across its sides. 'A couple of the boys are hanging,' confirmed penalty hero Dante Polvara when asked about the celebrations from the previous night. For the first time the parade would start at Albyn Place, travelling down Union Street, on to Union Terrace, Schoolhill, and

Broad Street, going past Marischal College before finishing at the Town House. The scenes that unfolded that afternoon were of a biblical nature. The red sea that had descended on Hampden the day before had made its way back north, quadrupled in size, and flooded the streets of Aberdeen. It is thought that over 100,000 people turned out to welcome home the history-makers.

The only time this mass of celebration parted was to permit the slow, triumphant passage of the bus bearing the city's new heroes down Union Street. It was a scene that would rival the great emperors returning to Rome after a successful campaign on the frontiers. The great wall of red waved and roared as the players and manager heaved the Scottish Cup aloft to the crowd time after time. A clear sky hung over Aberdeen, and the city's granite glistened in the sunshine. The trophy, draped in red and white, sparkled as it was carried through the streets, its gleam mirrored in the eyes of the ebullient onlookers below. 'Working at the parade was absolutely brilliant,' said Beth Wallace, who was canvassing fans for Northsound 1. 'It was such an amazing work opportunity to truly capture everyone's feelings. Interviewing the fans was incredibly easy because people spoke so readily from their hearts. Their pride just burst through in our conversations, and it's now one of my favourite days working in radio.'

It is no secret that Union Street, just like most high streets across the UK, has suffered a severe decline over the last decade, with the Granite Mile experiencing a significant increase in empty shop units. The once-thriving shopping thoroughfare continues to grapple with high vacancy rates, increased competition from Union Square and the lingering effects of the pandemic. On this day the contrast was stark.

The energy and vibrant red that crowded on to the street for the parade was staggering. Children climbed up lampposts to get a glimpse of their heroes and of a trophy they had never seen before. Even for the older generation, who had enjoyed many a Scottish Cup parade – albeit a long time ago – it was a struggle to keep the grins and, in some cases, the tears at bay. The bus edged down Schoolhill and then up past the historic Marischal College before stopping in front of the Town House. 'Sunday was incredible, and I've seen a few of these parades,' said Dave Cormack. 'The city has been through a tough time these last few years with the downturn in oil and gas. The parade itself was incredible. I walked around from behind the Town House; we'd got dropped off, and I had no idea what to expect. I walked around with my granddaughters Kyla and Skye, one in each hand, aged nine and seven, and when we walked around, we were blown away. Thousands of people were there, and it was a wonderful experience for the city to have the open-top bus parade. A hundred thousand people were in the city centre, and the ability for the players, Jimmy and myself to go on to the famous balcony at the Town House was just a wonderful experience.'

The expressions on the faces of the players and Jimmy Thelin told how blown away they were by the turnout. 'It's been actually a bit unbelievable,' Thelin told reporters. 'It's much bigger than I thought. We talk about why we do it, and it's for [the fans] to enjoy and be proud of the city and all people around Aberdeen and who belong to Aberdeen Football Club.' The so-often equable Swede was clearly enjoying himself. He had a shot on the ultras' drum at the door of the Town House, before posing for a picture holding the very flag that had been briefly confiscated by the police at

Hampden the day before. Shayden Morris, who had turned the cup final in Aberdeen's favour, said that it was the best day of his life. At the Town House, the players took it in turn to show the sacred silverware off to the thousands of fans amassed below – each one of them cheered and serenaded. The loudest reception of the day was reserved for Graeme Shinnie. None of the players understood what ending the 35-year wait for the trophy meant as much as Shinnie did – he had walked the streets of Aberdeen growing up as a boy. Now to see them buzzing after captaining his team to Scottish Cup glory was, in his words, 'a dream come true'. The glistening eyes of the skipper told just how much this meant to him. He and his team-mates had rekindled the passion of an entire region and delivered memories for a lifetime.

With the streets awash with people, Aberdeen's businesses recorded unprecedented levels of sales. 'If anything, it was busier on the day of the parade and much more lively,' said Kieren Joseph of the Foundry Bar. 'From 2pm until midnight, the place was rocking and everyone was in great spirits, celebrating away. From a business perspective, we had a record-breaking week, and during the game from two to 6pm is the most money the pub has ever taken. Saturday was a record day. Sunday was also huge, and one of the best we have ever had. We added £40,000 to our normal weekly sales, touching £60,000 in three days after tax, which is incredible!' At the Castlegate, Italian restaurant La Lombarda, usually shut on Sundays, decided to open its doors. 'We pre-warned the chefs on Friday that if Aberdeen won on Saturday, we would be open on Sunday,' Chantal Necchi told *AberdeenInspired*. 'When we got down on Sunday morning, the Castlegate and Castle Street was absolutely packed from early on. The atmosphere was absolutely electric. I knew it would be big, but I never imagined it would be quite as spectacular on Sunday.' Meanwhile, during the parade, the ice cream shop Mackie's 19.2 in the city centre experienced its busiest ever hour since it opened its doors in 2017. It was a momentous weekend for Aberdeen's businesses just as much as it was for the football club – the atmosphere across the city was electric. 'We went into a bar after and it was just rammed with Aberdeen fans,' said Michael Grant. 'Everyone was singing the European song and going mental. Someone came in with a big inflatable cup in his hand, and the place just roared, as if it had been Thelin himself coming in with the real thing. Everyone was totally joyous. I think, as Scots and Aberdonians, we all like moaning and grumbling about things. But on the rare occasions when it all comes together and the club wins something, it's a lovely feeling – it's special.'

Just as Jimmy Thelin and his charges had refused to acquiesce to the pre-written Scottish Cup Final script, the city shone out bright and proud in spite of those who like to paint it as otherwise. For those who continue to perpetuate the grey, dour misconceptions around Aberdeen and the north-east, their fallacies had been obliterated over two glorious days. For that weekend, the glittering Silver City, bedecked in red and white, was national news. 'I remember the night after the final, I caught a short clip on BBC News – maybe 30 seconds on the Scottish Cup,' recalled journalist Graham Spiers. 'They showed a few of the penalties, with that incredible red wall of Aberdeen fans behind the goal. I remember thinking, that looks fantastic – not just for Aberdeen, but for Scottish football itself. I've got lots of friends in London and across England, and I could just imagine them seeing that and thinking, wow – Aberdeen beat Celtic. That's something. It had that kind of impact. I think Aberdeen winning the cup was just brilliant for Scottish football. I could never get this corroborated, but I honestly believe that even someone like Brendan Rodgers would admit, deep down, that Aberdeen's win was good for the game here. I wouldn't be surprised if, at some point down the line, he even says as much – because it just feels true. It was refreshing.'

The circulation of newspapers may be ever increasingly on the decline, but, for that weekend, sales in Aberdeenshire boomed. In the way that supporters of all clubs do when their team hits the headlines, Sunday morning saw a flood of Dons fans rush to the local newsagent – keepsakes and clippings that would be passed on from generation to generation secured. 'I certainly think sports editors across Scotland would have gone into that weekend fully prepared for lavish treble coverage,' said Spiers. 'I'm pretty sure that was the mindset in newsrooms on the Saturday morning: Celtic are going to win, it's going to be a treble, we need to have pages and pages ready. Back page, inside double-spreads – the works. There would have been huge amounts of Celtic treble copy lined up. Even with all the anticipation of a Celtic win, I think a lot of newspapers would have been happy with an upset. Because, from a journalistic point of view, an upset is a gift. It's a brilliant story. I still remember watching Southampton of the Second Division beat Manchester United in the 1976 FA Cup Final – what a shock that was. And Aberdeen beating Celtic carried that same sense of surprise: refreshing, different, even unbelievable. So, I don't think sports editors would have been gritting their teeth or disappointed. Quite the opposite – they'd have been saying, this is fantastic. We've got a real story on our hands. And in journalism, a cup upset is always gold dust.'

Indeed, the back pages of all of the national papers featured Aberdeen; the parade scenes were visible on the home page of the BBC News website, and social media was awash with videos and images of the celebrations. Dave Cormack revealed that he received a personal letter of congratulations from Paris Saint-Germain president Nasser Al-Khelaifi, while the Frankfurt directors would celebrate the trophy win by opening the five-litre bottle of whisky Aberdeen had gifted them when the clubs had met in the Conference League in 2023. Motions were passed in both the Scottish Parliament and Westminster to congratulate the Dons on their Scottish Cup success, while Thelin hit the headlines back home in his native Sweden.

Aberdonians and anyone connected to the city or football club felt ten feet tall. The return of the world's oldest national trophy to the Pittodrie cabinet did more than end a 35-year wait – it reignited a deep pride, binding club, city and region together. If only for one weekend, it was a reminder that the Granite City and its people will not be overlooked, nor pushed aside, and will always have their place in the national story. Like the granite of its streets and the North Sea that beats against its coast, the people of the north-east endure. They stand firm and resilient. Hopefully, it won't be another three and a half decades before the scenes of that weekend in May return to the streets of Aberdeen. Until that day comes, 24 and 25 May 2025 will live long in the memory.

13

One of Our Own

'IT WAS frustrating after last year's cup final watching Union Street being packed with all of the fans that were celebrating. I want to experience that myself and go and win trophies and have an open-top bus down Union Street.'

Those were the words of Graeme Shinnie in 2015 after being officially unveiled as an Aberdeen player. His frustrations from that 2014 League Cup Final would have been quelled somewhat as he arrived at Pittodrie just days after lifting the Scottish Cup as captain of Inverness Caledonian Thistle. However, he now had his sights set on doing the same with his hometown club. Shinnie wasn't alive the last time Aberdeen won the Scottish Cup. Born in the Granite City on 4 August 1991, he was always destined to be a footballer. From a young age it was all he had ever known, ingrained into him by his older brother Andrew. Growing up in Cove Bay, the Shinnie brothers spent countless hours kicking a ball around the car park that lay at the back of their family home, their garden fence postulating as goals. In the same stereotypical vein as most older siblings, Andrew would force his little brother in front of the fence to act as a goalkeeper while he practised his shooting. Young Graeme accepted his role and actually admitted to aspiring to be a goalkeeper up until he was about nine years old.

However, his hopes of becoming a professional player looked to be dashed when he was diagnosed with Crohn's disease at age 12. Crohn's, a lifelong condition that inflames the digestive system, causing painful flare-ups and digestive problems, has a heavy impact on daily life for sufferers. With the prognosis it looked near impossible for young Graeme to follow in Andrew's footsteps and forge a career in the game. As would come to define the man, he persevered. Graeme was soon spotted as an impressive young talent and signed with Dyce Boys Club, renowned for their conveyor belt of local talent. Scott Booth, Russell Anderson, Stuart Armstrong and Andrew Shinnie are just some of the success stories to have cut their teeth at Dyce. Graeme shelved the idea of becoming a goalkeeper and quickly impressed in the middle of the pitch at Dyce, while attending Kincorth Academy in Aberdeen.

A self-confessed late bloomer, Shinnie continued to enjoy boys club football as his schooling concluded, even undertaking work experience at a car garage fitting tyres while exploring potential career paths. The decision quickly became an easy one as he was eventually picked up by scouts from Inverness Caledonian Thistle and lured north to sign his first pro contract with the Highland club in 2008. He initially joined the club as part of the under-17 cohort, and it was only then where his preferred position became left-back. However, before it had even begun, it looked as if his professional dream would be pulled from under him. With Inverness being relegated from the top flight at the end of 2009, the club made the difficult decision to scrap the under-19 team in a bid to cut costs. Only a handful of the players were kept on and fast-tracked into the first team – luckily, Shinnie was one of them. The Aberdeen loon wouldn't then have to wait long before he got his first taste of senior football, making his debut in a League Cup clash against Annan Athletic a few months later.

Shinnie's qualities were immediately evident; however, with limited playing opportunities, he was earmarked for a loan move to Highland League Forres Mechanics. 'I remember Caley Thistle phoned asking if we would be interested in taking Shinnie on loan,' remembered Charlie Rowley, who was the Forres Mechanics assistant manager at the time. 'We immediately said yes as Inverness were in the Championship at the time, so had a good standard of players. He came in on the Wednesday and we were due to play Cove, who were one of the best teams in the league at the time, at home on the Saturday. I remember the manager said it would be a bit soon to just throw him straight in for the match. I disagreed. I just said, "You've got nothing to lose. Just chuck him in and see. If he lasts an hour, so be it." So, we decided to play him at left-back. And he was absolutely outstanding that night – by far and away the best player on the pitch. We soon realised that we had a real player on our hands at that level.'

Forres Mechanics won the match 2-1 and Shinnie had made an immediate impression at his new club. Rowley said, 'He became a starter with us every week. His tenacity and energy made him stand out on the pitch, but particularly his fitness, which you needed to have as a left-back to be able to get up and down the pitch. The way in which he conducted himself was so impressive. How he integrated himself into the dressing room, you would have thought he had been with us for years.' It would go on to be a season to remember for Shinnie and the Mechanics as they lifted the Highland League Cup, defeating Rothes 2-0 in the final. 'We won that trophy without conceding a goal, and Shinnie played his part in that. He was at the forefront of the celebrations after we won the trophy and stayed with the whole team in Elgin. It was great to see a young lad who was so willing to dedicate himself to the club. We only gave him the platform at Forres and he more than grabbed it with two hands,' added Rowley.

After his successful spell battling it out in the Highland League, Shinnie returned to Inverness keen to break through into the first team. Despite the Caley Jags being promoted to the Scottish Premier League for the 2010/11 season, Shinnie's energy and tenacity earned him a regular starting berth at left-back. 'I didn't like Shinnie when he first came through at Inverness because he was so fit,' laughed Adam Rooney, who played with the young full-back in the Highlands. 'Terry Butcher, who was the manager at the time, used to like making us do some running training and Shinnie would be lapping me! He was one of the fittest players I have ever played with; it was just incredible how he managed to maintain himself.'

Shinnie impressed so much that Inverness offered him a three-year contract extension, which he signed in December 2010. It would have felt like Christmas had come early. And then, disaster struck. After playing the full 90 minutes in a Scottish Cup tie against Greenock Morton in January, Shinnie's Crohn's reared its ugly head. 'That game was the last straw,' he told Sky Sports. 'My parents had come up for the game, and I went home that night and broke down. I couldn't go on and the pain was too much for me. I had to have a bath almost every hour to relieve the pain.' Shinnie went into hospital in Inverness and, within a matter of days, he underwent a significant surgery that lasted 11 hours. When the doctors opened him up it was worse than first feared. Part of his bowel and colon was removed, and he had three abscesses, which had to be drained. It was a long road to recovery, and Shinnie's football career was put on hold, even admitting himself to not knowing whether or not he would ever be able to return fully.

Determined not to let the setback define him, remarkably, just five months after his major operation, Shinnie featured as a substitute on the opening day of the 2011/12 season. Over the subsequent years he solidified his position as Inverness's starting left-back while they established themselves in Scotland's top flight, achieving impressive finishes of fourth and fifth in 2013 and 2014, respectively. The latter was a significant season for Inverness as they reached their first major final, the League Cup Final, where they faced off against Aberdeen. 'It was a dreadful match,' recalled Adam Rooney. 'But the main thing everyone remembers is arriving at the stadium and just seeing red everywhere. The Aberdeen fans, of which there were about 40,000, were just amazing and I actually think it gave the players a bit of stage fright.' The Irishman would be the one to strike the winning penalty, sending the large Aberdeen support delirious but in the same breath breaking the heart of one of his former Inverness team-mates.

Shinnie found the defeat difficult to stomach. However, the disappointment only strengthened his desire to lift a trophy, and with John Hughes at the helm he was handed the captain's armband for the following season. 'I got very, very lucky when I went up to Inverness because I got Shinnie right at the peak of his powers,' said Hughes, unable to hide his passion for his former skipper as he spoke. 'You could just see he was bursting to learn more and more; he was like a sponge. When I initially went in and tried to change the playing style, you could see he was like "oh, what's this?" and wanted to know everything – he just loved it. The ambition was piling out of him. The way he trained, every minute of every day, set an unbelievable standard for everyone else. He epitomised everything good we did at Inverness. His fitness levels and his engine were unbelievable, and I honestly think he was every bit as good as Andy Robertson at the time.'

With Shinnie leading the team, it was a season of unprecedented success as they recorded a third-placed finish behind only Aberdeen and Celtic, qualified for the Europa League, and defeated Falkirk 2-1 in the Scottish Cup Final to lift the club's first major trophy. Hughes puts the team's success that season in part down to his captain, who he lovingly nicknamed 'Shinbone'. 'He was just constant, and he had a real desire to be the best that he could possibly be. Shinbone never had an ego and was always very humble and let his football do the talking. If he had something to say, he would say it, but he was always very positive. If you are describing him as a leader, he led by example; the way he trained, the way he conducted himself, and what he gave on the football pitch. Away from the pitch, he's pretty quiet. If there were games on or the reserves were playing, he would be up watching the boys. He was always supportive of anything that was going on at the club. He was all over it. He just wanted success. He would never be found wanting, ever. He's got that never-give-up attitude. In the Scottish Cup Final, I had to ask him to play right-back because David Raven was injured, and he immediately said, "No bother, no questions asked." He would do anything for the team. When you see your leader doing that and seeing he is up for it, then the rest of the players follow, and that's what he did for me.'

With the Scottish Cup secured, Shinnie departed Inverness on the highest note possible, subsequently joining his hometown club in the summer of 2015. Despite the success he had enjoyed at Inverness, arriving back in the Granite City was a step up – yet Shinnie was determined to carry his rich vein of form into his new surroundings. Just as he had at Forres Mechanics and Inverness, Shinnie quickly impressed with his work ethic and established himself as one of the first names on the team sheet at Aberdeen under Derek McInnes. In his first season he racked up 45 appearances, every one of them coming as a member of the starting 11. Shinnie epitomised the hard-working player, biting into tackles, the raw passion for the shirt he wore apparent, with a sprinkling of quality on top – the fans loved it. The fact that he was a local loon, born and raised in Aberdeen, only further ingratiated him to the faithful – he was one of their own. 'He is just the type of player that drives the rest of the team on,' said Rooney, who linked back up with Shinnie at Aberdeen. 'I remember playing against Hibs at Pittodrie. We were 4-1 up going into the 90th minute, and Shinnie was already on a yellow card. Hibs were breaking away from a corner on the other side of the pitch from where he was. He then ran 50 yards over to chop someone down and win the ball. My immediate thought was, "What are you doing?" risking the red card and missing the next game. But that's just who he is. His desire and leadership are unparalleled. While he has never been technically brilliant, he is a true leader, driving everyone on with his infectious energy.'

Shinnie's first cup final appearance for Aberdeen came in 2016 but ended in bitter disappointment as the Dons were routed 3-0 by Brendan Rodgers's Celtic side. However, the opportunity to right the wrongs of that dismal November evening quickly presented itself as Aberdeen marched into their first Scottish Cup Final since 2000 later that season. Only two years prior, Shinnie had lifted the trophy as captain for Inverness, and he was determined to do the same for Aberdeen. McInnes decided to hand Shinnie the armband for the huge occasion, given the rumours swirling around club captain Ryan Jack at the time. 'It's a big honour but it's not going to change the way that I play,' said Shinnie before the game. Despite a momentous effort from Aberdeen to topple an unbeatable Celtic they fell just short, Tom Rogic netting in the final minute to give the Hoops an unbeaten domestic treble – Aberdeen had finished runners-up to them in every competition.

With Jack departing at the end of the season, Shinnie was made club captain, just as he had been at Inverness – it spoke volumes to his character. Another successful year followed; a stunning goal against Apollon Limassol at Pittodrie in European qualifiers at the start of the campaign got life as captain off to a flier for Shinnie. The goal kick-started the terrace chant 'Graeme Shinnie, he's one of our own' from the Red Army, which he was delighted with, saying after the game, 'It was one of the best moments I've had at the club. A packed stadium singing my name, it is what it's all about.' The Dons went on to secure a second-placed finish for the fourth year in a row, while Shinnie started to get regular call-ups to the Scotland squad, making his full debut at the end of the season against Peru. Despite all of the adversities that he'd had to overcome, Shinnie had scaled the international summit and pulled on a Scotland shirt to represent his country. He didn't rest on his laurels; he wanted more. 'He wants to win everything,' said former team-mate Joe Lewis. 'In every single session, he's competitive – snapping into tackles, working hard, doing whatever it takes to win, even in the smallest five-a-side games. He's a fantastic professional. He's not someone who smashes the gym or stays behind after every session, but he leads by example and drives training. Of course, coaches set the structure, but ultimately, it's the players who set the standard – and he does that better than anyone. He brings energy and enthusiasm every single day. As a senior player and now as captain, he's a brilliant example. That's what leadership is. Not just what you do on a Saturday, but what you do every single day.'

Shinnie never shied away from his desire to win silverware with Aberdeen, and after the Dons once again lost out to Celtic in the 2018 League Cup Final it appeared as if those hopes had been extinguished for good. He had played in and captained the best Aberdeen side since the turn of the millennium but they had been unfortunate to run into Brendan Rodgers's dominant Celtic along the way. The career of a professional footballer is a short one, and the pressure for players outside of the elite level to make as much money as possible to provide for their families' future is significant. With an international cap under his belt and impressing regularly for Aberdeen, some fruitful offers soon came in from England. Derby County, managed by Frank Lampard at the time, came calling, and Shinnie had a tough decision to make. He openly admitted to loving Aberdeen, but wanted to test himself down south and, at 27 years old, felt like this would be his last opportunity to do so. It was announced by Aberdeen before the end of the season that Shinnie, despite the club's best efforts to keep him, would join the East Midlands club in the summer of 2019. Shinnie, although not 100 per cent fit, was determined to play in what would be his last game at Pittodrie and strapped up his ankle for the penultimate game of the season against Hearts. He captained the side to a 2-1 win and got a rousing send-off from the home crowd, who showered him with plaudits and appreciation for all that he had done in red – even if he hadn't lifted any silverware. It would be something that would continuously rankle with him.

Shinnie's stint south of the border was a whirlwind that quickly developed into a disaster. Frank Lampard, who had sold the Derby dream to Shinnie, moved on to Chelsea in the same summer, and he found himself quickly out of favour and unfancied by new manager Phillip Cocu. As the new season got under way, Shinnie started dropping out of matchday squads altogether and even considered getting a loan move out of the club he had just joined. It was a horrible beginning to what was supposed to be an exciting new era. After showing the grit and determination to fight for his place, Shinnie forced his way back into the starting 11, only to then get the first serious injury of his career – a hamstring tear which sidelined him for 12 weeks. On his return, he had only just got back to full fitness when the COVID-19 pandemic forced football across the globe into shutdown. It felt like he couldn't catch a break. The 2020/21 season offered some respite, with Shinnie playing almost every game and being named Derby's player of the year as they narrowly avoided relegation. But the following campaign brought financial collapse and with it a 21-point deduction that doomed the club from the outset. In January 2022, Shinnie was reluctantly sold to Wigan Athletic for the club to bring in some much-needed cash, and he helped the Latics secure promotion, albeit amid limited playing time.

When the opportunity to head back north presented itself, it was a decision he had no qualms over. The pull of Aberdeen and the chance to play a leading role again proved too strong to resist. Shinnie spearheaded the Dons' impressive run to end up in third spot and secure guaranteed group-stage European football, a first for the club since 2008. Having initially joined from Wigan on loan, Shinnie secured a permanent return to the north-east that summer, not wanting to pass up the opportunity to lead a Euro tour across the continent. 'My full focus was always on returning here,' said Shinnie after completing his permanent move. 'It's a club I love.'

With Shinnie back, he was immediately installed as captain once more, and there was a sense that things had fallen back into their rightful place. The Dons reached the final of the League Cup and the semi-final of the Scottish Cup in his first full season back at Pittodrie – it felt as if he had picked up exactly where he had left off, albeit the league form was rather disastrous. Still, however, silverware in red eluded Shinnie. With the arrival of Jimmy Thelin in the summer of 2024, you could have forgiven the midfield spoiler for feeling slightly apprehensive, given his recent experiences of managerial turnover during his stint in England. However, any fears were quickly assuaged. 'Graeme is an amazing captain,' said Thelin in his first few weeks in the job. 'The first weeks here, how he pushes the young players in a good way, how he showed his leadership when we travel or after the training sessions, he is a really good leader for the team.'

With the captain's pride of place firmly secured, Shinnie once again made no secret of his aims for both himself and his team-mates for the season. 'The determination to try to lift silverware at this club has always been massive for me,' wrote Shinnie in his captain's column in the new season's first matchday programme. 'I'm desperate for it. I'd love to win a cup and we came pretty close last season with one final and a Scottish Cup semi-final that will live long in the memory. But we don't want to be a side of nearly men, we want to go one better and bring a cup home. It's been too long.' Nobody understood that quite as much as Graeme Shinnie. During his two spells at the club, he had played in four finals for Aberdeen, all of them ending in defeat. But Shinnie did what he does best in the face of disappointment. He persevered.

Shinnie led Aberdeen out on to the Hampden pitch for the 2025 Scottish Cup Final ahead of his 300th appearance for the club, an unbelievable landmark for someone whose footballing future had hung in the balance more than once during the early stages of his career. But here he was, taking his hometown side out on to the biggest stage of them all for a second time. When asked before the match if he viewed this final as his last shot at winning a trophy with the Dons, he said, 'Yes. It's very difficult to get to finals so you've always got to view them as a last chance.' This was it then, one last shot at glory. One last chance for Graeme Shinnie to etch his name into history. If this was going to be the day that Shinnie lifted the trophy for the Dons, he would need to overcome seemingly insurmountable odds to do so. However, he has never paid any heed to the odds.

After a herculean 120 minutes in the middle of the pitch, Shinnie stepped up to take Aberdeen's first penalty of the shoot-out. He slammed it into the top corner and clutched at the badge on his chest, laying to rest his 2014 League Cup Final demons. It was a penalty of exquisite quality. As ever,

Shinnie set the tone, leading by example. Polvara, Dabbagh and Palaversa all subsequently hit the net and Aberdeen were on the brink. As Dimitar Mitov made the cup-winning save, Shinnie sank to his knees inside the centre circle, both arms raised to the sky, tears in his eyes. His journey was complete. It was the end of a long road, scarred by heartbreak and humiliation. Six times Shinnie had trudged off the pitch at Hampden following defeat to Celtic, yet here he was now, a Scottish Cup winner with Aberdeen.

Watching on in the stands was Charlie Rowley, the former Forres assistant manager and a season ticket holder at Pittodrie: 'It's funny how things work out in football. I was just filled with pride and elation to see somebody that you've worked with lift the cup for your boyhood team. I can't help but smile when you think about it.' John Hughes, Shinnie's former manager at Inverness, was delighted: 'I would do anything for the wee fella. To see him lifting the cup for Aberdeen, his hometown club, was absolutely unbelievable. He deserves it. We're all mates in the game, but I would say you get about ten guys in football you come across and think "he was one of the real good ones". He is one of those – and I'm not talking about football ability; I'm talking about a right good lad and a brilliant guy to work with.'

The emotion poured out of Shinnie. Ten years on from winning the trophy with Inverness, he had done it again, becoming the first player to win the Scottish Cup as captain of two different clubs. As he climbed the Hampden steps, Shinnie followed in the footsteps of the fabled quartet of Aberdeen skippers who had come before him: Frank Dunlop, Martin Buchan, Willie Miller and Alex McLeish. There would need to be space made for the addition of one more name to that list. With a nod to the indomitable Miller, who was watching on, grinning in the stands, Shinnie ended Aberdeen's 35-year wait for the Scottish Cup by lifting the trophy with one hand, the other outstretched. 'Nobody deserves it more,' said former team-mate Joe Lewis. 'He is Aberdeen through and through and has given his all for the football club. To see him lift that trophy was unbelievable. I couldn't have been happier for anyone.'

It might have been ten years since he had first joined Aberdeen back in 2015, but Shinnie would finally fulfil the dream of parading silverware down Union Street that he had harboured since signing for the club. The captain had woven his own legend into the fabric of Aberdeen Football Club; he would be part of its story for eternity – a heavenly dancer in red, chasing across the Aberdeen sky for evermore.

14

The Road Ahead

FOR AS long as anyone could remember, the great yearning of the Aberdeen support was to see the Scottish Cup return to Pittodrie. Now, at last, they had realised the dream. The cup was won and, standing at the pinnacle, the storm clouds parted and the sun shone out brighter and clearer than it ever had before. Life had never felt so good. If this were a fairytale the story would end. 'And they lived happily ever after.'

But football is no fantasy – its stories never truly end – and the tale of Aberdeen Football Club swiftly moves on. As the cup-winning party spilled into the following week, and indeed the summer beyond, it was already back down to business for Pittodrie's top brass. 'Even though we won, on the Monday morning after the cup final, we actually started planning,' said chairman Dave Cormack. 'The players went off, Jimmy went off, but there was some planning going on for [the new] season. That included the things we've done at Pittodrie, like getting the huge big screen, redoing the flags outside the main stand, and a number of other things, including filling the holes with new Perspex at the Richard Donald Stand, which looks a bit odd, but don't worry, all that's going to get sorted out.'

Testament to the courage of their convictions, it would have been the exact same process should the cup final have ended in disappointment. Cormack said, '[SFA chief executive] Neil Doncaster, behind me, tapped me on the shoulder when it got to penalties and just said, "I don't know how you cope with this." I said, "Well, Neil, look, it's going to be what it's going to be. If we win these penalties, it's fantastic. If we lose them, we'll dust ourselves down, and on Monday morning, we'll start getting ready for next season." For me and my family, our satisfaction comes from trying to put a smile on the city's face through the club and through the Community Trust, and the other charities we support, because we've been blessed financially. So, my reflection [on the cup final] was more on being so pleased for the club and supporters. We've had people working there for decades who haven't seen us win the Scottish Cup, some people for 30 years. So anyway, it was more of a reflection for a few days, and then on with it for the next season.'

It would be fair to say it has been a rollercoaster for Cormack since taking over as chairman in 2019. The number of cases of whiplash in the north-east has considerably increased among those trying to keep track of the Dons' league position over the early part of the 2020s. On the pitch, stability has been hard to come by, the team flipping between being world-beaters one moment and posting record winless runs the next. It's no smooth ride following Aberdeen. As a result, Cormack has had his doubters, but what cannot be questioned is his fervour and ambition to make the club the best version of itself. He said, 'Behind the scenes, the support I've received from the silent, vast majority around Aberdeen is truly encouraging and keeps you going. Listen, nobody is immune to criticism, because you have to listen. It's a responsibility for me. Even before I took it on, I got back involved as a director in June 2017. So, [my involvement] started right after the last Scottish Cup Final we lost to Celtic in 2017. Behind the scenes, I spent most of my time helping reorganise the club and in readiness to maybe take over. It has been over eight years now, and close to six years as chairman. However, while you see the chairman talking to the press, there's a whole board and an executive team running things day to day. I'm not heavily involved in the day-to-day operations. Clearly, at certain times of the season, decisions need to be made on buying players and the like; you never get a player for what you think you're going to get them for! It's similar to things like Cormack Park, where we're looking to install an indoor pitch. These things take time.'

Off the field, there is no doubt that the club has come on leaps and bounds since business-savvy Cormack took the reins. Turnover is at record levels, commercial and retail income is on the up, the Pittodrie matchday hospitality suites have been given an impressive facelift, AberDNA was launched and members are at a record high, while season ticket sales have increased by 35 per cent. It's positive mood music when it comes to the business side of the club, and will continue to be so given Cormack's personal track record – he sold his clinical software solution company for £567m in early 2016. While maximising income streams will help stabilise the club and keep the wage-to-turnover ratio low, Aberdeen's true differentiator and path to becoming a top European club lies in mastering player trading. They have made an impressive start. Under Cormack's chairmanship they have raked in over £20m in player sales – more than Hearts and Hibs combined over the same period. The acquisition and subsequent sales of Ylber Ramadani and Bojan Miovski for a combined profit of nearly £6m is the gold standard of what Aberdeen are now trying to achieve. But, in order to sustain the self-inflicted loss-making model which the club is pursuing, they need to be bringing in big transfer fees on a regular basis. In this environment there is no time for self-satisfaction, and the focus quickly moves on to unearthing the next undiscovered gem.

Since Nuno de Almeida, former sporting director at Rio Ave in Portugal, stepped into the role of head of recruitment in December 2024, Aberdeen have doubled their scouting network and now employ full-time scouts in Scandinavia and southern Europe. Cormack has been inspired by a handful of other clubs on the continent: 'The clubs that obviously come to mind at different levels [that we take inspiration from] are Nordsjælland, Bodø/Glimt, and even AZ Alkmaar in Holland. Many of these clubs, including Elfsborg during Jimmy's six years there, have successfully implemented player trading. With the model that we are now working with you always have to be on the lookout for what's next. Current players may have opportunities to move elsewhere in the future. Hopefully, this would result in a significant reward for the club, which would then be reinvested – that's the model. So, we need others coming in. This is one of the reasons players choose to join our club; they could have gone to other teams that might have paid them more. But they come for the opportunity as we give players a chance, and we facilitate their progression, similar to successful approaches by other successful clubs. Many players who have moved on are performing well at their new clubs.'

All of that is contingent upon the fact that signing a large proportion of project players is only tolerable to supporters if the results on the pitch remain positive. The new model is still in an early stage at Aberdeen, and time will tell whether it will be a success. Largely of its own volition, Aberdeen has now established itself as a club that players can use as a precursor to making the move to one of Europe's top leagues; elsewhere in Scotland, there has been a sharp increase in the number of multi-club ownerships as clubs look to leverage the knowledge and databases of bigger organisations. Brighton owner and professional gambler Tony Bloom bought a 29 per cent stake in Hearts for £9.86m, the Black Knight Group and Billy Foley bought a 25 per cent stake in Hibernian for £6m, while a consortium comprising the 49ers Enterprises – majority owners of Leeds United – and American tycoon Andrew Cavenagh completed their £75m takeover of Rangers. Does Aberdeen risk being left behind? 'There's a lot being said about the investment going into some of the other clubs,' said Cormack. 'My friends and I have invested £25m over the last eight years, including recently, where we invested another £8m. However, I prefer that we keep a low profile with it, rather than being out there saying we are going to do this, and we are going to do that. I still think it's very early days in our understanding of multi-club ownership. A lot of people are running to it. The core idea is economies of scale, particularly in areas like scouting and other operational efficiencies. However, success ultimately depends on the quality of the individuals involved. While I have a long association with Aberdeen Football Club, I'm proud that throughout our entire 122-year history, it remains locally driven by Aberdonians. One can never say never to future opportunities. We don't know how European football will evolve. I believe domestic leagues will be under real threat, with significant money and sponsorships shifting to the new European competitions and the guises that they come in, such as the new Champions League format. I believe significant changes will occur in Europe over the next five to ten years. As a club, we need to be positioned to be part of that, whatever form it takes. We'll see an increase in multi-club environments. But as a club, we've been using algorithms and data analytics for player recruitment for six years, so it's not new to us. So, I believe time will tell on that front.'

However, the core of any successful player trading model is bringing through talent from an academy, something Scottish clubs have struggled to do on a regular basis. Aberdeen are not immune to the issue: throughout the 2024/25 season they were ranked as one of the worst clubs at giving opportunities to players aged 21 or under, with just 7.9 per cent of all league minutes going to the supposed next generation. Further to that, only one of the Scottish Cup Final starting 11 was a product of the Dons' youth setup – even if it was a formidable performance from Jack Milne. It's an issue the club are aware of and something they have moved to address. In the summer of 2025, Aberdeen welcomed David Lawrie, former chief operating officer of the Right to Dream Academy, to the board as a non-executive director. Right to Dream, set up as a charitable football academy to create pathways for young African football talent around the world, is one of those multi-club, multi-academy groups operating in Africa, Europe and the US, with professional teams including FC Nordsjælland in Denmark, FC Masar in Egypt and San Diego FC in MLS. Nordsjælland narrowly missed out on the league title in 2023 by just four points and the following season delivered a positive player trading surplus of over £40m – a quite incredible achievement for a club which averages attendances of under 5,000. Aberdeen were looking to tap into some of that magic.

'Dave Lawrie, who is now one of our directors, was instrumental in the entire Nordsjælland group, including Right to Dream Academy, serving as chief operating officer before retiring,' said Cormack. 'His insights have been a big help in our analysis and strategy.' Lawrie's experience no doubt helped shape the strategic changes to Aberdeen's youth pathway, which were announced in July 2025. The club has overhauled its academy structure in a bid to get a better return on its £2.2m annual investment by helping young players transition more effectively into the first team. A key change is withdrawing from the Club Academy Scotland under-19 competitive programme; instead, the focus will be on the CAS under-17 format, plus loans, cooperation agreements and bespoke game programmes to give top young players senior-level experience earlier. This will be supported by a new transition coach role to bridge the gap between academy and senior football. Cormack explained, 'We're already seeing the benefits of young players going out on loan. It's like going back to the future, because that's how all the players came through at Aberdeen back in the day – Willie Miller, Alex McLeish and Steven Glass all went out on loan to junior, Highland League, and lower division clubs to play men's football. So, we'll continue to evaluate this model, but you also have to be practical. You need a core team of experienced players.'

No one illustrates the positive impact of early exposure to senior football better than Graeme Shinnie. The current captain's loan spell at Forres Mechanics gave him the platform to get regular game time in full-blooded Highland League clashes, and he never looked back. The promise of first-team football for academy starlets is something that Aberdeen will need if they are to hold on to their stars of tomorrow. The impact of Brexit, and the end of the freedom of movement for European workers, on English clubs has made it much harder for them to attract top young talent from the continent to bolster their academies. Instead they are now sniffing north of the border, and the impact has been keenly felt by Scottish clubs. Fletcher Boyd, Cammy Wilson and Ellis Clark are just some of the recent names to depart Pittodrie for England. The money that English clubs cough up for their academy stars completely dwarfs anything that Aberdeen would be able to offer. The only riposte for clubs like the Dons in the face of this bottomless well of money clubs in England have to pull on is that they can offer young players a guaranteed pathway to the first team – something which is highly unlikely to transpire at clubs down south.

Time will tell whether the focus shift will increase the readiness of the youth players to make the step up into the first team, but a conveyor belt of young talent is a necessity should Aberdeen look to progress as a club. Within those upper echelons across Europe, the successful clubs they should look to as the benchmark tend to share four key pillars: a smart player trading model, a strong youth development system, a clear and consistent playing philosophy, and a modern, fit-for-purpose stadium. Aberdeen have made strides to improve in three of those areas; however, the new, state-of-the-art stadium, visions of which the club has harboured for decades, still feels no closer to being realised. Pittodrie, despite the nostalgia that it conjures up, is a great drain on the club's resources. 'We have to invest in Pittodrie to be involved in Europe,' said Cormack. 'There is a constant need

to improve the stadium, like the lighting, where we spent
£100,000 on improved lighting for the South Stand. Even if
we move stadiums, by the time we get planning permission
and construction is complete, it will be six or eight years.
So, we are planning to do what we can at Pittodrie. The
real legacy I, or we as a board, would like to leave is a new
stadium. I'm still convinced, and many people, even on the
council, agree that we need to regenerate Aberdeen. This is
because renewable energy jobs will not come to Aberdeen if
companies have a choice of location. They will go somewhere
where the shopping and leisure experience for employees'
families is paramount; otherwise, they can't attract staff.
Currently, in Aberdeen, there's a real lack of leisure facilities
because everything behind the beach ballroom is closed or
has been knocked down. So, the legacy I'd like to leave is
for the club to be part of a regeneration of Aberdeen that
provides facilities for Aberdonians for the next 50 years and
beyond that allows the city to truly become the renewable
energy capital that politicians are advocating for.'

In the aftermath of the cup final, Cormack penned a
passionate open message, calling on politicians, business
leaders and other stakeholders to come together to deliver
a community stadium along with best-in-class sports and
leisure facilities that will attract and retain people in the
city, creating jobs and prosperity. An independent study,
funded jointly by the club and the council, revealed that the
economic uplift from such a facility would be £1bn over 50
years. In a bid to bring stakeholders back around the table,
Cormack has said the club is willing to offer up the land
on which Pittodrie currently sits in order to get proposals
for a new beachfront stadium back on course. While there
will be those who will be happy to see Aberdeen cling on

to Pittodrie for as long as possible, the truth is that it is fast becoming a relic from a forgotten era, even if it is a beautiful one at that. A stadium is the beating heart of any club: the place where fans and players unite, and the stage on which the club presents itself to the world. As Aberdeen strives to modernise in every department, a state-of-the-art home is a necessity. Without it, much of the excellent progress being made risks being undermined.

While a resolution to the stadium stalemate is being developed, Aberdeen should focus on making headway on the continent. It is no exaggeration to say Scottish teams have had a dismal time of it in European competition since the turn of the millennium. Over the last 25 years, only once has a club outside of Celtic and Rangers qualified for the knockout phase of a European competition since 2000 – Jimmy Calderwood's Aberdeen in 2008. With the creation of the Conference League in 2021 and the changing formats from groups to leagues across all the UEFA competitions, the opportunity has never been greater to make headway in Europe. Djurgårdens of Sweden and AZ Alkmaar have both reached the semi-finals of the Conference League – the former operating with a turnover similar to that of Aberdeen. It should not be outside the realms of possibility for Aberdeen and Scotland's other top clubs outside of the big two to aim for something similar. At the very least, the Dons need to be qualifying for the league phase of the Europa League or Conference League every other season. It's a difficult task from the current position, especially given the fluctuating national coefficient, but if the club wants to become a serious player in Europe then it's where it needs to be.

While that is the ultimate goal, at times, it couldn't feel further away than it has at certain points over the early to mid-2020s, with the club cycling through several managers and years of turbulence. A period of stability, which involves consistent top-end of the table league finishes, is absolutely crucial to allow the club to lay the foundations for those four key pillars. Cormack said, 'Look, we won the Scottish Cup, and we should see that as a platform to drive forward. I wouldn't say the Scottish Cup is a distant memory, but we're in the here and now. We'll take it, we'll be thankful for it, we'll never forget it, but you know, it's looking to the future which is now our focus.'

Every morning, Cormack takes some time for himself when he wakes up. In those quiet moments of reflection, does he dream about an Aberdeen squad littered with young Scottish starlets walking out in a European quarter-final at a brand-spanking new stadium at the city's beachfront? It's the end goal. For that dream to be realised, there's a long, long road ahead. Saturday, 24 May 2025 will have felt like the pinnacle for supporters. But, as one peak is conquered, a higher summit comes into view beyond. The Scottish Cup was only the beginning. The journey doesn't end here, and if Aberdeen want to build on the trophy success, as Cormack says, they have to view this as the beginning of a new era.

15

That Day in May

HOW ABERDEEN build on their Scottish Cup triumph remains to be seen. In the unforgiving world of Scottish football, setbacks are inevitable. There will be more highs and more lows, players will come and go, and one day Jimmy Thelin's time in the dugout will draw to a close. Yet whenever that moment arrives, regardless of the circumstances, he will leave the north-east a legend. For the players who contributed to that unforgettable day, they will for ever be etched into the club's history. Saturday, 24 May 2025 was the apotheosis for supporters of Aberdeen Football Club. From the ashes of the heartbreaks, humiliations, and near misses, the Dons sprang from the shadows to meet their day of reckoning with intrepidity. The old kings of Scotland were crowned once again. A whole generation of fans has been raised on the tales and feats of the old heroes and legends of the north-east. *The best defender in all of Europe played in the red of Aberdeen? The greatest manager the world has ever seen led the Dons as they slew the great Real Madrid?* It is scarcely believable, in the ilk of folk tales. But now that generation has its own fable to tell – the day a red horde marched south, turning what seemed a hopeless expedition into one of the greatest triumphs in the club's history. They struck down the foe that had been the root of so much heartache over the last 35 years and carried the glittering Scottish Cup back home for the first time in three and a half decades. It was Aberdeen's ultimate redemption. Red redemption. Scottish Cup winners again, finally.

Bibliography

Books:
Ferguson, A., & McIlvanney, H., *Managing My Life* (London: Hodder and Stoughton, 1999)
Grant, M., *Fergie Rises* (Edinburgh: Polaris, 2024)
Reid, H., *The Final Whistle* (Edinburgh: Birlinn, 2005)
Webster, J., *The First 100 Years of the Dons* (London: Hodder and Stoughton, 2002)

Newspapers:
Borås Tidning
Daily Mail
Daily Record
Dundee Courier
Evening Express
Grampian Online
Press and Journal
The Sun
The Times

Websites:
Aberdeen FC matchday programmes 2024/2025
AberdeenInspired
AFC Heritage Trust

BBC
FBREF
Footballxg
Identity Hunters
Official Aberdeen FC website
Open Goal
Premier Sports
Red TV
Sky Sports
Transfermrkt